LIVES FOREVER
CHANGED

My Spiritual Adventures
With The Lord

PAT BARRETT

Library of Congress Control Number: 2023922814

ISBN: 979-8-9885572-0-3 (Paperback)
ISBN: 979-8-9885572-1-0 (E-book)

US $14.95

DEDICATION

I dedicate this book to my wife Rebecca,
my children, grandchildren and future generations
to come. I pray my entire family will receive
Jesus Christ as their Lord and Savior and
be His close personal friend.

I'm confident my experiential stories will
encourage you to follow Jesus Christ with a deeper
understanding of His love, presence and power
through the Holy Spirit. He resides in you and
desires to work through you to love, bless and
pray for those around you.

Remember, the spirit realm is real and you are
sent here to accomplish His kingdom purposes.

Have fun on your spiritual adventures with the Lord!

TABLE OF CONTENTS

INTRODUCTION

I primarily wrote this book using experiential stories within stories to answer some of the questions I have received from family, friends and church members regarding supernatural manifestations that suddenly pop up during prayer ministry. If you pray, fast, ask, hunger and expectantly seek the Lord for the desires of His heart, He will use you to minister to the hearts and minds of others. Remember, the Lord respects everyone the same. When you make yourself available, you'll be totally surprised by who you'll meet, through divine appointments, and how the Lord will use you to bless and speak His heart to them. He not only convicts and changes their heart but also captivates yours to become more like Him. One bit of advice... find and attend a spirit-filled church with pastoral mentors who will encourage and train you.

Prior to 1991, I was totally oblivious to ministry and power evangelism with the demonstration of signs and wonders. This reality changed super fast. Thankfully, the Lord gave me three great pastors as mentors who moved powerfully in the gifts of the Holy Spirit. This definitely caught and held my attention as my spiritual adventures were just beginning. After seeing and experiencing the supernatural power of the Lord, my spiritual hunger led me to attend every ministry training class offered at my church. The pastors teaching the class encouraged and challenged us to pray and minister to at least 100 people. They gave us permission to make mistakes and encouraged us to never be afraid, believing our questions would be answered by the Lord.

I also learned the meaning of, "If you catch'em, you clean'em." Thankfully, the pastors doors were always open if I had any unanswered questions or needed advice on how-to minister healing to individuals with deeper spiritual issues.

In this book you'll read how my life quickly became a fantastic journey full of adventures with the Lord as He opened my eyes to the spiritual world around me. My experiences are not intended to provide a formula for prayer ministry, rather to serve as a reminder to keep your hands in your pockets, assume nothing and ask the Heavenly Father what He wants you to say or do through Christ Jesus, as the Holy Spirit leads. Always be ready for unexpected responses as the light of Jesus in you exposes spiritual darkness. Go into the harvest and be His power evangelists!

CHAPTER 1

A REVELATION OF CHRIST'S AUTHORITY IN YOU

In this chapter:

- Discover How Deep the Heavenly Father's Love Is for You!
- Know Who You Are and Experience the Father's Love
- It's Time for Spiritually Awakening with Understanding
- Relationship! Relationship! Relationship!

Discover How Deep the Heavenly Father's Love Is for You!

Remember, Jesus Christ the anointed one lives in you! (1John 2:27). I'm amazed to hear of the many mental and spiritual struggles people go through in order to experience and receive a revelation of the deep, passionate, consuming love of their Heavenly Father (Isaiah 53:4-5). His true love will penetrate all mental blocks and become an overwhelming life changing experience.

Today, a large part of the Church is short-sighted — they only learn about the Father's love for them. See, you have to believe and catch the revelation of Him and His love for you and own it in your heart. It's only after you've experienced the overwhelming, heart-to-heart, spirit-to-spirit, totally heart-penetrating, eyes-tearing, emotional, beyond-knowledge love... you'll realize and understand how deep, how merciful, the Father's love is for you. Immersed in His love, your heart becomes one with His for a moment, an hour, a day, a month... and eventually forever. I'm always saying, "More, Lord!" (1 John 4:9).

As you become consistently mindful of Him every day you begin to see differently, through His eyes. You begin to think differently, with the mind of Christ (1 Corinthians 2:16). And you talk differently, out of His heart. You walk differently — full of His presence and authority (Luke 10:19). You become a vessel of His love, light, glory and honor!

Our Heavenly Father's intense love takes you deeper and deeper as He continually heals and consumes hidden hurts and wounds in your body, soul, and spirit. The spiritual world opens up before you as His light and His love shines through you. He'll bring people to you who need His love, His healing, His freedom.

You'll find a new level of boldness and confidence in Him when you speak and minister out of His heart. The fear of taking risks in ministry will disappear when you expect His love to manifest upon others as you pray for them. When you minister out of your heart or out of love — and not your head, you will see things happen. But then when you minister out of the Father's heart, seeing and understanding His perspective on things, you will see major things happen! Remember, you are not responsible for the results, He is.

But we are responsible to be obedient to His heart and to be a vessel of His love. I often say, "Stretch out your hand and see what happens!" Jesus Christ the anointed one lives in you and He operates through you. As you minister and pray for someone, imagine His hand on the person instead of yours. It will increase your faith; you'll be expecting to see something happen. Ministering the Father's love through Jesus Christ is an exciting adventure! And His next divine appointment for you is right around the corner.

Know Who You Are and Experience the Father's Love

It's important to remember, God has poured out all of His love in you (Romans 5:5). There is no need to ask for "more love." Do you find yourself asking, "Why don't I feel any different?," or "Why don't I feel all of His love in me?" Ask the Lord to remove anything in you that is covering up His love in your heart. Give the Lord permission to reveal whatever is in you that is covering up His love — sin, unforgiveness, negative vows, self-hatred, jealousy, idols, etc. Once you repent and change, obey Him. His love will gradually be uncovered and begin to shine in and through you more brightly and powerfully. And as you experience more of His love, your heart wounds will be healed. If darkness is present, it will leave, or be consumed in His presence. It's important to ask the Father's love to fill every empty void in our heart especially during and after ministry. His love crowds out darkness replacing it with His light 'Presence'.

While ministering the Father's love, the light of Jesus' presence in you causes darkness or demons to immediately leave, or they expose themselves in words or gestures. *Please note: I refer to demonic spirits as darkness and vice versa throughout the book.* Do not be afraid of them manifesting. Jesus Christ of Nazareth protects you from demons who want to challenge you physically or spiritually. *More on this later*... Jesus is the one who removes all stumbling blocks before you and He is your rear guard.

I've learned through experience we don't need to bind demons during ministry. Demons are already bound in the presence of Jesus Christ, the Anointed One, in you. It's important to catch this truth in your heart. Demons will recognize you know who you are in Christ and the authority in you comes from Him! In other words, they see Christ light in you and know you belong to Him (2 Corinthians 4:6). You don't cause demons to reveal themselves. The presence of Christ and His light in you causes this to happen. Actually, I would say 80% of tormenting darkness leaves a person without them knowing by standing in the manifest presence of the Lord, or by having a short revelatory conversation before the actual prayer begins. Any remaining darkness may be stubborn to leave since it may be connected to a past or present sin, unforgiveness, a curse, the occult, or other reasons. If demons manifest while you are ministering to someone, it means they recognize Jesus Christ in you and they know He is going to use you as His anointed vessel to set the captive person free. Don't ever be afraid. In over 30 years of ministry, demonic entities have always cowered. They obey because they recognize the presence, power and authority of the Lord Jesus Christ in me.

As you speak, they tremble before you (James 2:19). The manifesting darkness hears Jesus Christ of Nazareth's loud commanding voice coming out of your mouth in the spirit, and they tremble. Own this truth as a reality in faith, because it's true.

When you invite Jesus Christ into your heart, accept Him as Lord and Savior, ask Him for forgiveness of all your sins and invite the Holy Spirit to come in — you become born-again in the Spirit. Your body becomes the temple of the Holy Spirit. In that moment, you are no longer born of this world, you are reborn spiritually from above, from His kingdom. Although you live in this world, you are not of this world spiritually anymore (John 15:18-19, John 17:14-16). You were sent here with a purpose and a destiny (Ephesians 1:11). Jesus resides in you and you are filled with power of the Holy Spirit WITHOUT MEASURE (John 3:34). This gives you the authority to powerfully operate and advance the Kingdom of God and fulfill the great commission Jesus called you to (Matthew 28:18-20, Acts 1:8). You are no longer your own. You are set apart from the world and He shows you favor in His purposes. You are redeemed by Jesus' precious Blood. You are bought with the price of His Blood, death, and resurrection (1 Peter 1:19). You totally belong to Him. You are betrothed to Him as part of the body and the coming bride of Christ (1 Corinthians 12, Revelation 19:7-9).

Early in my journey with the Lord I wore a ring that I blessed and dedicated to Him as an engagement ring, a betrothal ring. It reminded me of Jesus' passionate love for me, and my love for Him, especially when darkness came to tempt me. I still remember situations when looking at the ring on my finger helped me not to sin against Him. I had to choose who's desire I was going to follow, mine or His. I didn't want to rebel against Him or hurt His heart. More importantly, I didn't want to turn away from Him and choose sin as if I was kneeling and worshiping the enemy with my back toward the Lord. Over time, I discovered as long as I sought Him and allowed His love to capture my heart, the desire to choose Him and abide in Him grew and became more and more naturally part of me. If you are truly in love with a person, you will not willfully sin against them. If you fall in love with the Lord, willfully sinning against Him will become a non-issue in your life. The Lord says, if you love Me, you will keep my commandments (John 14:15). The Spiritual gifts and His anointing will automatically start operating through His love connection with you. Ministry will become more exciting as you surrender and allow His love to speak through you and change lives.

It's Time for Spiritually Awakening With Understanding

Unfortunately, many churches don't teach about the manifestation of the gifts of the Holy Spirit. Or worse, they don't believe they are relevant today. Sadly, church and community outreach programs have become more important and now their church members don't even know how to release the presence and power of the Holy Spirit within them to fulfill His commission (See Matthew 28:16-20). They may be saved by God's grace, baptized, and filled with the Holy Spirit, but they exhibit a case of Holy Spirit amnesia becoming complacent with an abundance of head knowledge. This knowledge lacks the life-changing, experiential, powerful manifestation of the Holy Spirit through them.

There's a lot of misunderstanding concerning effective "power evangelism" ministry. I rarely hear anything spoken about this most important but sadly missing ingredient. What's missing is the cognitive, heart-felt, deeply in-love relationship with our Heavenly Father through Christ Jesus. Remember, Jesus came to reveal the Father's love for us (John 17:25-26)! His love is the light and power that heals and transforms lives.

Many people pray, "Father... in Jesus' name," but they usually don't see any manifestation of His powerful love through signs and wonders. I believe this happens because a person's mind is more focused on speaking His name in prayer without the heart-felt love and compassion moving His heart to touch the person receiving ministry. People pray for more power not realizing the source of His loving power (being released through them) is found in an intimate love relationship with Him (the anointed one) in their hearts. It involves His complete ownership and our utter dependency on Him. Deep manifesting Holy Spirit power = a deep love relationship. Deep calls to deep (Psalm 42:7).

Some church leaders ask, "Are you willing to pay the price to walk like Jesus in His anointing?" What they don't realize is the cost becomes your pleasure and desire when you are in love with Him. Ask Him, "Lord, help me to truly fall in love with you. I want to know and experience your love for me." As you pray for His wonderful manifest love, truly desiring it, hungering after it, even taking time to fast frequently, receiving and believing in your heart to connect with His heart, you will fall deeply in love with Him. In this short time, He'll draw you to Himself. He'll draw your heart to His heart.

Relationship! Relationship! Relationship!

It's like He hugs you so tight that you can feel His heart beating, your hearts begin to beat in unison. "Draw near to God and He will draw near to you" (James 4:8). Tears will flow down your cheeks. He will become so tangible, so real, so comforting, so inclusive that His presence around you will feel far-reaching. He brings your heart experientially into a different place – where your mind can barely catch up. Your senses are heightened. You are suddenly highly aware. This love relationship quickly grows in your prayer closet. It is enhanced in the secret place. Greater intimacy, understanding, and revelation from His perspective will develop in your heart and in your life when you spend time with Him. You'll know what matters to Him. You will begin to love what He loves, and hate what He hates, and He gives you understanding.

Tears will well up in your eyes for others over their simple concerns. Sometimes you can't even speak His name, "Jesus", because just thinking His name floods your heart and you feel like crying before you can speak it out. It's happening right now as I write this.

The Lord usually ministers to my heart at the same time He uses me to minister to others. Often when I speak a message from His heart to theirs, my heart is instantly touched. I struggle to hold back the emotional tears as His presence becomes at times overwhelming.

The Lord reveals the hearts of men and women to you so He can use you to speak His words convicting their hearts in love, not in condemnation or judgment, concerning any sin in their lives He reveals by his Holy Spirit. Ask the Holy Spirit to teach you how to pray and minister effectively and powerfully.

Remember, The Holy Spirit is your teacher and comforter. You don't want your words and prayers to be like a sounding gong (1 Corinthians 13:1). You may want to fast and pray so your prayers will be zeroing in like a rifle shot and not all over the place like a shotgun blast. You want your prayers to be short and effective. Don't pray "preaching" prayers. Jesus ministered powerfully, using few words and achieving amazing results. Through Jesus you can do the same. Life with Him is an adventure and a challenge. He takes your heart deeper and deeper into His well of living waters and reveals the secrets of the Heavenly Father's heart to you.

Sin becomes a non-issue in your life because His love reigns in you. If you fall short and sin, forgiveness is a breath away. His desires become your desires. Obedience to Him becomes a pleasing virtue in your life. …Walking with my Friend, my Lord, my Savior, my Heavenly Father, and the Holy Spirit has been a great testimony of His unending love to the hearts of His children He places before me.

CHAPTER 2

JESUS CHRIST – THE VICTORIOUS WARRIOR

In this chapter:
- Capture in Your Heart – We Are One in Jesus
- We Are More Than Conquerors in Christ Jesus
- Common Manifestations and What They May Reveal

Capture in Your Heart – We Are One in Jesus

Jesus is a Victorious Warrior in your midst (Zephaniah 3:27). He demonstrates His power and reveals all deceptive and demonic games.

During prayer ministry demons shouting or causing someone to throw up is not encouraged. Just because someone throws up, doesn't mean they are set free. This is a common misconception and deception demons use to make it appear as if they are leaving or have left the person. In truth ninety percent of the time they haven't gone anywhere. They are just hiding. Sometimes a weaker spirit may be pushed out by the stronger manifesting demon in an attempt to trick everyone into thinking it's gone. You can ask the person receiving prayer if the demon has left or is still there. They usually know.

In the kingdom of darkness there is an army of dark spirits with ranks similar to the U.S. military like captain, lieutenant, sergeant, private, and so on. One major difference is they are not loyal to each other and operate somewhat chaotically in their own will. Of course, Satan is in charge, but he can only be in one place at a time. He is not omnipresent like Jesus. So a manifesting sergeant may push out a private during deliverance and the sergeant may try to hide to keep itself from being expelled. An experienced prayer minister will discern this and deal with the enemy's deception accordingly. As Christians, we're the Army of God. We are more than conquerors because Jesus Christ defeated Satan and his dark ones at the cross (Colossians 2:15, Romans 8:37). It's very important to remember this truth if darkness manifests during prayer, they have already been defeated by Jesus victory on the cross. Our weapons are not of this carnal nature, they are spiritual (2 Corinthians 10:4-6).

One time I witnessed a woman tell her pastor the demon was still there and she could feel it. She had just received prayer. The pastor said, "No, it's not, sister. You just threw it up and you're free of it." Meanwhile, the woman wasn't free of anything other than her lunch and continued to struggle with the demon's destructive work in her life. The deceptive demon, along with its cohorts, tricked the pastor into thinking they were gone when they weren't.

Sometimes the person feels a little better after receiving partial deliverance but unfortunately it doesn't last long. If the person doesn't receive complete prayer ministry, eventually the dark spirit of lower rank and less strength returns to the root cause of the stronghold. It usually returns to where it had been pushed out. For example, when someone is sexually abused (root cause), the trauma may be covered with guilt or shame. Yet underneath, there is a sea of anger, rage, self-loathing, condemnation, and unforgiveness. They work together to create a fortress to protect and hide the original root resulting in a stronghold. It's not unusual for the person receiving prayer to be super embarrassed or ashamed to speak out details related to the initial root cause. Or they may have mentally blocked out the memory altogether. This is one reason why praying for symptoms may bring temporary relief but usually ends with the expelled spirit(s) in time, returning and reattaching to the stronghold.

We Are More Than Conquerors in Christ Jesus

I'd also like to mention, praying in a loud voice doesn't make your prayers any more effective or powerful. There is no need to shout at the person receiving prayer or at a manifesting demon. With the authority of Christ in us one can whisper and darkness must obey. If there is no remaining legal hold, the darkness will leave. Remember the enemy is already defeated (Luke 10:19). Be mindful of this truth as you are ministering.

Jesus cuts to the chase and speaks through your mouth. When you speak the manifesting demons and their cohorts hear His loud, earth-shaking voice. Sometimes when you speak, you'll notice the person who is receiving ministry will begin to tremble or shake their head while they make a face and turn away. I've seen this occur in many situations. And no, it's not bad breath. Often, a person's eyes will roll back and their eyeballs are completely white. The manifesting demon cannot look at the bright white light emanating from your Christ-like eyes. The cause of this could be sin like unforgiveness, or a hurt, or connection to the occult, etc. Usually the Holy Spirit reveals it to you quickly through the spiritual gift of discernment or a word of knowledge (1 Corinthians 12:10). If you don't discern anything, take some time and ask the person a few questions: What do you feel or see? When did this begin? And so on…

When the eyes roll up appearing half-white, unforgiveness from a hurt is usually the issue. In this case, you can't cast out a harbored hurt. Take a few minutes to ask the person if they are having a difficult time forgiving someone. They usually know the answer. But if they can't think of anyone to forgive, pray with them and ask the Lord if they need to forgive anyone. You'll be surprised how fast the Lord will reveal the answer and the hidden memory pops up. Sometimes, the person may need to forgive themselves as well for past or present issues. It's important to take the time to lead them in a repeat-after-me forgiveness prayer. (See sample Forgiveness Prayer in the Appendix)

Make sure you keep your eyes open and look at the person you are praying for. Your prayers aren't any more powerful with your eyes closed than with them open. If they're closed, you'll miss seeing any physical manifestation the Holy Spirit is using to reveal what's on the surface and you'll miss even deeper issues the Lord wants to heal.

It's not necessary to verbally call out everything you sense that may be the cause or root issues the person is spiritually dealing with. You can whisper a command to a suspected dark spirit to reveal (manifest) itself in some way in Jesus name, and observe what happens. Jesus' authority is the same regardless of the volume the command is spoken. However, it is important when praying about sensitive issues to use caution and not assume, guess and speak out thoughts that may embarrass the person receiving prayer, especially when praying in a team. We don't want the person to feel embarrassed or feel exposed and resist prayer for personal issues in the future. Always be sensitive and use wisdom when praying for someone.

Common Manifestations and What They May Reveal

I will briefly explain how the Lord led me to pray and minister to each person. Remember, the Lord is the healer and the deliverer. He wants His children healed and free. You are an ambassador of His love, a son or daughter of the King of Kings.

1. Quivering lower lip and/or chin
    - This usually reveals healing/deliverance is needed for childhood issues and/or trauma.

- Have the person look at you while you pray a blessing over their childhood. Bless them from conception in their mother's womb and dedicate their childhood to the Lord.

- Don't rush. You don't have to discern everything. Be like Jesus and ask questions. Here are a few examples:

  1. Are you feeling or seeing anything?

  2. Has the Lord brought up any thoughts or memories?

  3. What kind of childhood did you have?

  4. Did you experience any childhood trauma? And so on...

- Break the power of all negative words spoken over them from conception in their mother's womb. Proclaim the blood of Jesus over all negative words stuck in their heart and command them to fall to the ground powerless in Jesus' name. Then ask the Lord to fill every void with the Father's love.

- See what happens next and follow the leading of the Holy Spirit. He's your teacher and guide (John 14:26).

2. Rubbing hands nervously together as if they are being washed or scrubbed clean

   - This usually reveals that healing and/or deliverance is needed for past or present personal guilt.

   - Ask the person if there is anything troubling them in their life making them feel guilty or dirty?

   - You may have also need to break the power of negative words spoken to them as a child, including being in their mother's womb. Sometimes a person receives blame for something they did or didn't do and feels guilty.

   - See what happens next and follow the leading of the Holy Spirit. He's your teacher and guide.

3. Teeth chattering or feeling a chill or cold

   - This usually reveals healing/deliverance is needed for unforgiveness, a curse, practicing witchcraft, or dabbling (involvement) with the occult, or a demon is manifesting in fear because they see Jesus Christ in you.

   - Don't rush. Take some time and ask a few questions to help narrow down the root of issue:

- Do they see, feel, or hear anything? Some examples include:
  - Did they ever use a Ouija board?
  - Have they ever made any negative vows?
  - Have they ever participated in a ritual? (Some examples include séances, necromancy, invoking familiar family spirits, Joan of Arc rituals, blood covenants, drinking potions, or using white or black magic.)
  - First, lead the person in a repeat-after-me Salvation Prayer, even if a salvation prayer was spoken in the past. Ask the Lord to forgive them for all of their sins. Have them renounce, rebuke, and break the power of anything of darkness (in Jesus' name) that may have attached itself to them concerning this issue. Then command it to go directly to Jesus Christ of Nazareth for Him to deal with. (See Salvation and Forgiveness Prayers in the Appendix)
- Ask the Holy Spirit to fill any voids with the perfect love of Abba Father. His love will begin to crowd out any residue of darkness.
- See what happens next. Follow the leading of the Holy Spirit. He's your teacher and guide.

4. Shaking their head slowly back and forth as if they're saying, "No"
   - This usually reveals healing/deliverance is needed from a lying spirit that is speaking to the person while you are praying. It's denying them the Lord's blessings. It may be related to a spirit of unworthiness that God doesn't love them or they can't be forgiven. Some secretly believe the lie that they have committed the unpardonable sin.
   - I ask the person to look at me as I speak. "The Lord says 'Yes' to you in every way." Sometimes their head will shake back and forth even faster. If this happens, I continue to say, "Yes." He says, "'Yes" to you. He loves you.'" Sometimes they start to cry as they continue to shake their head back and forth. This is usually a breakthrough related to the pain or unbelief they have been carrying for years. Or the Lord has convicted their heart concerning past issues.
   - Sometimes the enemy closes the ears of the person so they can't hear a word you're saying. They may look at you strangely as if they are trying to understand what you are saying. If this happens, ask them if they can hear you. If they don't respond and they continue to look at you strangely, put

your hands on their ears simultaneously and break the power of a deaf and dumb spirit in Jesus' name. Ask the person, "Can you can hear me now?" The answer should be, "Yes."

- If the person continues to shake their head back and forth with no response, you'll need to rebuke and break the power of a lying spirit and command it to be silent. Ask them what they are feeling or hearing. Break off the spirit of fear and release the Lord's peace and truth. Dedicate their mind, thoughts, dreams, etc. to Jesus Christ and bless them with His peace from head to toe.

- Be aware (in general) that many people change their first name, given at birth, to a Christian name of their choosing. Their birth name may be hard to pronounce or reminds them of past extensive trauma. Usually they take a new biblical first name and feel renewed as a person. This new name doesn't releases any darkness on the spiritual side. Be mindful their true (given at birth) first name can be cursed or have a demonic presence attached to it, or actually be a demonic name. It's a good hiding place and can demonically influence the person, but more powerfully when the name is spoken. I have experienced this very often in other countries, but many people are moving around these days. Have the person look at your eyes then bless their birth name and break the power of any curses, spells, witchcraft or demonic incantations spoken or released upon it, and themselves in Jesus Name. Make sure you speak out their name precisely because the enemy is legalistic. If you mispronounce their first name, the darkness spiritually has a legal right to stay. I also would plead the blood of Jesus over the old name and their new Christian name.

- See what happens next. Follow the leading of the Holy Spirit. He's your teacher and your guide.

5. Eyes burning with exaggerated blinking or darting around as if they don't want to look at you

- This usually reveals healing/deliverance is needed for a spirit of fear (and its cohorts) that has gained access through their eyes, or possibly a demon has been pushed to the surface to be dealt with.

- Have the person look at you. Sometimes darkness will manifest, and the person will be unable to look at the light you radiate from your Christ-like eyes. They may even say, "It burns!" Ask them to keep their eyes open and look at you. Pray, bless and dedicate their eyes to Jesus Christ of Nazareth. Command everything of darkness to come into the light. Break the power of sin, trauma and/or fear they may have received through their eyes. If they blink quickly for a moment and then can see you clearly it usually means the attached darkness has left. They usually feel it leave. They should now be able to look at your eyes without a problem. The person may need to be led in a prayer of forgiveness for looking at something they knew was sinful (such as pornography) or forgive someone from their past.

- Ask if they are seeing, feeling, or thinking about anything in particular. Maybe they watched a very scary movie and a spirit of fear entered through their eyes. These may be clues revealing root issues that can be prayed for next. See what happens. Follow the leading of the Holy Spirit. He is your teacher and guide.

Flickering or fluttering eyelids, tingling, heat, or electricity on face, hands or entire body, breeze blowing over fingers or through hair or in ears, crying, laughing, or being slain in the Spirit — these are some of the manifestations of the Holy Spirit. Many people have never experienced the manifest presence of the Holy Spirit, so they may get nervous or afraid. Pray and break the power of the spirit of fear trying to rob the blessing of experiencing and acknowledging the Holy Spirit's presence upon them.

As the Holy Spirit brings things up, all forgotten sins will eventually need to be confessed to Jesus. He forgives all confessed sin which cancels the enemy's legal right to stay. With a blink of an eye the enemy has to leave along with all of its cohorts (friends).

Now ask the Heavenly Father's love to fill the place where the enemy once occupied in their heart that belonged to darkness and replace it with Jesus' bright light. This crowds out any hidden darkness and pushes other sins/darkness to the surface to be dealt with in the same way, possibly another time.

Jesus says, "Be holy as I am holy." (1 Peter 1:16) Be aware within weeks or months after a person is set free from sins of unforgiveness, the occult, and so on, darkness may seem to reappear. It doesn't mean the same issue is back. The love and presence of Abba Father is working and going deeper to expose any root in their heart that is causing residual sin/darkness to be pushed up to the surface to be dealt with.

There are so many manifestations of the enemy I recognize from experience. Setting the captives free is a pleasure and it's exciting. Seeing lives change before your eyes is a true blessing! And actually, deliverance is easy if the person wants to be free. The real work begins after getting free — rebuilding, changing habits and making healthy decisions.

CHAPTER 3

MY FIRST DEMONIC ENCOUNTER WITH A SPIRIT OF FEAR

In this chapter:
- Lessons in Spiritual Authority and Overcoming
- My Son's Encounter with Fear: Breaking Its Power and Experiencing Instant Life-Changing Results

Lessons in Spiritual Authority and Overcoming

It was 1991. I had just returned home after attending my first three-day Holy Spirit conference and was heading to bed. Little did I know I was about to get a lesson in spiritual warfare and experience the manifest power of God in a tangible way.

After falling asleep the Lord woke me up. I felt fearful that a stranger was in my house, so I immediately got out of bed and stood up. Then I felt this intense tingling in and on my body. I was looking around my bedroom and suddenly the wall in front of me moved back about ten feet in the spirit realm. In an instant, a short, black demon about 2 ½ feet tall came running through the wall toward me. It looked like its stubby legs were going hyper-fast, but its body was moving much slower towards me.

My heart started beating faster but then I heard a voice off to my right say, "Speak these words to it." I don't remember the words verbatim, but it was along these lines, "In the name of Jesus, I command you to get out of here!" I didn't know what else to do so I obeyed and spoke the words as instructed. Surprisingly, as the words came out of my mouth, they were ear-piercingly thundering loud, causing everything in and around me to vibrate and shake intensely.

The black demon crunched up like a paper bag and flew backward super-fast through the wall at the Lord's rebuke. My body was still trembling observing the results and I remember saying to myself, "Wow, that was the Lord's voice speaking through me."

Then all of a sudden, another short, black demon came running through the wall toward me. This time the Lord told me to say the same command as before but to point my finger at it first before I spoke. I was a little less afraid this time and thought, "Well, I guess it's my turn to speak since His voice spoke before." So, I lifted up my arm and pointed my finger at the demon running toward me and I said, "In the name of Jesus, I command you to get out of here!" Again, to my amazement, the Lord's voice came out of my mouth and it was as loud as before. The intensity of His voice sounded like ear piercing cracking thunder and an extremely loud earthquake ripping the ground open simultaneously. It felt like it shook everything in and around me. My body was trembling so intensely it caused my arm and finger to move upward. From my vantage point, it looked like the demon was stuck to the end of my pointed finger, but at a distance.

Again, instantly the demon was crunched up like a black paper bag and flew backward super-fast making another exit hole in the wall about five feet up from the floor — exactly where my finger was pointing. I remember thinking, "Wow, it was His voice again that spoke my words." I was super excited and realized the Lord was using this experience to teach me.

About 30 seconds later while I was still facing the wall and calming down, I said, "Come on back sucker. I'm ready for you now." I was pumped and expected another demon to run toward me. But to my disappointment, the wall moved back towards me to its original position. I heard His soft voice say to me, "I'll never leave you or forsake you." (Deuteronomy 31:6) All of the tingling left my body as I stood next to my bed. I was blown away!

I thought to myself, "More, Lord. That was cool!" The next day I told a church friend about the experience and he directed me to read Luke 11:20, "But if I drive out demons by the finger of God, then the kingdom of God has come upon you." I didn't know this was a scripture at the time, but it made me excited to learn more.

It wasn't until a year later I realized the voice that spoke through me that night was the voice of my Heavenly Father. *I will explain more about this revelation later.*

When it was all said and done, I remember standing in my room with my confidence soaring through the roof. I concluded that demons hear the Lord's voice through us as we speak and He really does the battle. I remember hearing some of this taught at the three-day Christian conference, but when I experienced it, I owned it! Simply learning about something is trivial compared to learning through experience. You typically don't forget what you experience!

After this, I petitioned the Lord to use me to set the captives free. I fasted, prayed, and asked the Lord for divine appointments. And wow, He sent them to me. It became a ministry. The manifestations became really intense as the Holy Spirit continued teaching me. The Lord was giving me divine appointments everywhere. Really cool!

The following Sunday I spoke to my pastor and told him about my experience in the bedroom. Keep in mind, I had only been attending this church for 1½ months when this happened. I hadn't attended any church for 14 years before this time. He smiled and asked, "What kind of spirit was it?" I said, "I don't know, a short, black one with stubby legs." As he was still smiling at me, he asked me what I felt before it manifested. I said, "I felt super afraid someone was in the house while I was lying in bed that night." Then he asked me, "Did you ask the Lord, what it was?" I said, "No, not directly." Reflecting on my Catholic background, I thought to myself, "Right, the Lord isn't going to speak to me that way!" Months later I had a totally different perspective because of what I was taught and continued to experience.

The manifestations increased tremendously as the Lord continued teaching me to walk, stand, and speak in His authority releasing His children from the dominion of darkness…with Jesus always manifesting and revealing His presence.

My pastor explained that from now on I should ask the Lord the following questions before asking him any questions.

1. Lord, what is it I'm sensing or feeling?

2. What are you speaking or showing me?

3. What kind of spirit is it?

4. What do you want me to say or do?

He also told me the Holy Spirit was identifying the darkness or demon (in my bedroom that night) as a spirit of fear by using the spiritual gift of discerning of spirits (1 Corinthians 12:10). The pastor went on to say the spirit of fear may have come to rob the blessings from the three-day Holy Spirit retreat we attended or this spirit was hanging around me or the house and needed to be dealt with. As we grow closer to the Lord, His presence reveals what is around us or what is around others in the spirit realm.

He said, "the darkness could be testing you, but the Lord will use this opportunity to teach you." He added, "Always remember fear is a spirit. Fear doesn't belong to you, nor is it a part of you." It is written, "I do not come to bring a spirit of fear, but of love, power and a sound mind" (2 Timothy 1:7). You can renounce, rebuke, break the power of fear and its cohorts and command them to go, in Jesus' name.

The pastor went on to tell me a person can receive a spirit of fear from a personal trauma, watching scary movies, generational curses, decorating with demonic tribal masks, etc. Fear acts as an open door in the spirit which allows other darkness to come in and attach itself in some way.

My Son's Encounter with Fear: Breaking Its Power and Experiencing Instant Life-Changing Results

When my son was about 11 years old, he started attending a new school and was afraid to get on the bus. As far as we knew he didn't have any problems with other kids or teachers, but he definitely felt afraid on the bus and at school. Because of his intense fear we began to drop him off at school and pick him up each day. He stopped riding the bus.

Two weeks later while I was at work I finally came to my senses as a thought popped into my head – he was being tormented by a spirit of fear. I knew the Lord revealed this to me. That night we prayed over him in Jesus' name and rebuked a spirit of fear along with all of its cohorts/buddies and any familiar spirits. We also sealed any open doors in the spirit with the blood of Jesus Christ, any open doors where fear may have traveled through. I also asked the Father to summon a captain warrior angel to be with my son and do all of his spiritual battles.

The next morning, he actually wanted to take the bus because he didn't feel afraid anymore. He not only got on the bus to go to school, but he even rode it home at the end of the day. He was super excited to tell us he didn't feel afraid on the bus or in school anymore – this was a big deal! During this time, we noticed a remarkable change in him not only concerning the school bus but in other areas of his life as well. Even friends and family noticed a big change in him. He had increased confidence and surety. He wasn't afraid anymore.

When we told them he was set free from a spirit of fear, some of them believed but not everyone thought it was possible. They couldn't accept the truth. What can I say other than it's written, "…But God chose the foolish things of this world to confound the wise" (1 Corinthians 1:27).

CHAPTER 4

SECRET SIN EFFECTING THE CHURCH

In this chapter:
• Your Eyes Are the Window to Your Soul

Your Eyes Are the Window to Your Soul

You can also receive a spirit of lust and perversion through your eyes, the windows to your soul (Matthew 6:22), by willfully looking at sexually enticing images like pornography. Repeated exposure can lead to a cycle of sinful, habitual lusting in your heart and mind. Unfortunately, some church members and leaders are ensnared by this captivating, secret sin. Unless the Lord's presence exposes this lustful spirit or reveals it to a discerning member of the church, this spirit will hide while it effectively hampers the manifest presence of the Holy Spirit in the person's life and their church ministry. Sometimes their addiction is exposed when it comes into the light of Jesus while they are receiving ministry for other issues.

The Lord forgives a confessed sin, but we have to remember He is Holy. An unrepentant heart without conviction will not want to confess or receive ministry because of the embarrassment of 'stepping down' from their ministry during the healing and restoration process. Or maybe they love their sin more than bringing it before the Lord.

While counseling and ministering to people who are ensnared by the sin of pornography, they are usually totally unaware of the Lord's displeasure and how this hurts His heart. They are also unaware of the intense grip the enemy has on them. Many say, "I have it under control and can handle it." But when they decide to quit they have a rude spiritual awakening and realize they're hooked (addicted) and it's out of their control.

The Internet plays a key role in seducing innocent people, young and old, to take a quick look. They are totally unaware of what this spiritual and physical trap of darkness is capable of. It captures their mind, heart, and soul – eventually damaging everything and everyone. Married couples report feeling "cheated on" when it comes to their sex-life if their partner is watching porn. Divorce rates double concerning this issue. It's important to seek counseling, healing, and restoration.

CHAPTER 5

JESUS DOES IT ALL

In this chapter:
- The Lord Is Looking For Available, Teachable Vessels
- Salvation Prayer

The Lord Is Looking For Available, Teachable Vessels

I have hundreds of ministry stories that testify to super-powerful, mind-blowing Holy Spirit encounters of God's love and light, causing darkness to manifest in people He places around me. I've discovered the power of stories and how easily they are remembered compared to a teaching lecture. My prayer is that the Lord uses these true stories to minister to you personally. I believe they can teach you, equip you, and build your confidence to help you love and serve the people He brings to you for ministry or friendship.

Before telling you another story, I'd like to talk about a common ministry mindset I've encountered that limits the work of the Holy Spirit and hinders healing and lasting freedom.

Aside from those who don't believe the gifts of the Holy Spirit are for today, some ministries and churches don't or won't consider inner healing, including deliverance, as an option to help someone with deep spiritually rooted issues. They provide general counsel along with a few scriptures hoping to fix what ails the person including their thinking and habits. This is good however, many people have deep-seated issues like habitual sin, unforgiveness, past occult practices, victimization, or negative vows, and other issues giving darkness (demonic spirits) permission to establish strongholds or to partially torment or control areas of their life. Without identifying, repenting, renouncing, and rebuking the darkness, the afflicted person is usually unable to become truly free. And if they experience freedom, they'll need to be aware the darkness is angry about being evicted and will try hard to get back what it has lost with increased temptation. But as the person continues to resist the devil, he will flee (James 4:7).

In ministry it's always a good idea to begin with a prayer of agreement giving the Holy Spirit permission to reveal everything (memories, sin, vows, dreams, traumas, etc.) necessary for healing and freedom. It's important to ask the person <u>not</u> to pray as they are being ministered to. It can distract them from hearing the ministry prayers and possibly affect the depth of the Holy Spirit's touch to uncover and reveal issues of their heart.

A common ministry mistake is made when prayers are rushed and focused primarily on obvious symptoms instead of seeking the root cause. The person may experience some relief, even believing they are healed. But typically, it is short lived and they find themselves seeking prayer for the same issue week after week, month after month.

It's important to slow down and follow the leading of the Holy Spirit who will lovingly expose the root cause, open door or hook that is the source of affliction. Once this is revealed, lasting healing and change is possible.

I recommend taking a few minutes to interview the person and find out when the issue(s) first started. What was going on in their life at that time? Did they experience any trauma or life-changing events like divorce, death of a family member, loss of job, sudden illness, or financial crisis?

Let me say it again. Slow down. Don't rush. Wait on the Lord and the Holy Spirit. It may seem like it's taking a while, but without a doubt, the Lord will bring up what's necessary to reveal the access point where darkness (the enemy's hook) started its work in the person's life. They may also unknowingly start to manifest what the Lord wants to reveal.

Sometimes when a person begins to repent, the enemy may manifest by growling or cursing in an evil voice. The enemy wants to prevent the person from repenting. They know if the person confesses, repents and renounces, they will lose their legal hold and have to leave when commanded to go. The person receiving prayer is typically shocked at the realization they are no longer in control of their words or someone else's voice is coming out of their mouth. Their eyes will show how frightening this experience is as they desperately look to you for help.

Now… This is when you talk to them calmly to reassure them everything will be fine. The first thing I ask the person is, "What is your name? (If not known)." Then I ask, "Are you saved?" or, "Have you asked Jesus into your heart as your Lord and Savior?"

If darkness continues to manifest, I command it to be silent in the name of Jesus Christ of Nazareth. I command it to let the person speak to me. At this point I have a short reassuring conversation with the person and have them ask Jesus into their heart even if they say they are already saved. On several occasions, I've seen both proclaimed Christians and non-Christians unable to speak the name of Jesus. So I start by asking the person to repeat-after-me the following prayer:

Salvation Prayer

Part 1: Lord Jesus, come into my heart. Be my Lord and Savior. Forgive me for all of my sins, even the hidden sins in my heart that I'm not aware of and fill me with your Holy Spirit, right now, in Jesus' name.

Part 2: And I command any and all spirits of darkness who come to torment me in any way to hear what I speak right now in the name of Jesus Christ of Nazareth and I rebuke any disobedience. I rebuke and renounce all spirits of darkness and their cohorts that I have invited upon myself knowingly and unknowingly. I don't want you anymore. I don't need you anymore, I renounce you and command you to leave all parts of my life and go directly to Jesus Christ of Nazareth for Him to deal with you. I command you never to return to my life in Jesus' name. Jesus Christ of Nazareth is my new Lord and Master. And I give you, Lord, permission to remove anything that is not of you.

I added Part 2 to this prayer because it saves a lot of time and it is very effective. Sometimes it totally releases the person from any darkness attached to them on the surface and it can even expedite future deliverance if needed.

Sometimes, as a person repeats the Salvation Prayer they won't be able to say "Jesus." The enemy quickly manifests and prevents them from saying His entire name. The person struggles trying to say, "Lord Jeee…, Lord Jeee…, Lord Jeee…" and in their fear, which is really the enemy's fear, I tell them, "It's okay. Try to relax. Don't worry. You're fine. Look at my eyes and calm down." Then I break the power of the spirit of fear. I tell them I'm going to speak something else, in a minute, after they calm down.

The following declaration I speak is very important to understand and is very effective. It works great in deliverance issues, but it isn't limited to that area of ministry. This prayer is also excellent when darkness tries to prevent a person from verbally confessing, repenting and renouncing any sin before the Lord.

I have them look at my eyes and say, "In the name of Jesus Christ of Nazareth, I proclaim the blood of Jesus over the eyes and ears of the enemy to keep them from hearing or seeing this conversation." Instantly, the person can look at me and easily repeat every word of the entire Salvation Prayer without any interference.

Now comes the fun part! I ask the Lord to allow the enemy to hear every word the person just spoke. Parts 1 & 2 of the Salvation Prayer and everything else that needed to be confessed, forgiven, renounced and released through "The Blood Of Jesus". It takes about ten seconds for the enemy to hear and realize the following:

1. This person became born-again or re-dedicated their life to Jesus as their Lord, Savior, and Master.

2. They repented and asked for forgiveness for all of their sins. This releases any demonic legal hold because of confessed sin.

3. They renounced all powers of darkness they have invited into their life, knowingly and unknowingly.

4. They confirmed they no longer want or need the darkness or its cohorts anymore in their life.

5. They commanded all of the darkness and its cohorts to go directly to Jesus Christ of Nazareth for Him to deal with.

Once the enemy fully grasps what just happened the demon(s) or the enemy will immediately leave 80% of the time. Sometimes the person may quickly shake or shrug their shoulders indicating the afflicting dark spirit has left.

The other 20% of the time the process varies. For example, after realizing what the person prayed, Part 1 and Part 2 of the Salvation Prayer and other commands, a demon (darkness) can manifest abruptly with the person's eyes flared wide-open and looking shocked, along with their head shaking slowly back and forth, muttering gibberish followed by a few lingering "No's." The manifesting demonic expression on the person face often looks afraid and surprised at the same time. When this happens I smile and say to the manifesting darkness, "You have been renounced in Jesus' name and now Jesus is their Lord and Master. You have no more authority here. I command you, in the name of Jesus, to go and not return, right now!" A quick shocked look on the person's face follows and the darkness leaves. I smile in amazement.

Occasionally, you may encounter a very stubborn, angry, rebellious dark spirit struggling to stay. In truth it is fighting a losing battle trying to hold on as it appears to be sucked off the person. In a gurgling voice they sometimes say things like, "This is my home, you can't rebuke me!" I just smile and say, "bye bye!" Then they leave and disappear as if an angel yanked them away.

If the struggle lingers any longer, I ask the Heavenly Father to summon captain warrior angels to come and remove the renounced rebellious spirit. In an instant, the evil spirit (darkness/demon) is gone. Heavenly warrior angels don't mess around. When the spirit leaves, the person usually cries tears of relief. They are amazed how real the spirit world is. The person may express an experience of feeling light and peaceful. Their surroundings may visually appear brighter!

To test the results, I have the person say, "Lord Jesus, come into my heart...." and they have no problem repeating His name. I tell them that a few minutes earlier their spiritual father was the Devil, but Jesus Christ of Nazareth is their Lord and Savior now. Now you are saved!" I also tell them, Jesus continues to protect them as they continue to choose Him and Jesus says, "Go and sin no more so that all will be well with you" (John 8:11). Usually the healing and new Godly revelations within them continues for a few days. Sometimes past wounds from deep-seated unforgiveness, or abusive occult practices, will need additional prayer ministry to be resolved. The Lord tenderly unravels and heals all those who come before Him.

There are other ways to minister to someone in a similar situation, but this type of ministry teaches the person the following:

1. The spirit world is real and actually exists.

2. They can exercise their authority in Christ by asking for forgiveness, renouncing the darkness that was attached to them, and command it to leave and not return. Remember to ask the Heavenly Father to release his love into every void within the person. In this moment there is a great exchange – darkness is commanded out while His perfect love is received within.

3. Sin gives darkness permission to attach and afflict their spirit, soul and body.

4. Jesus is the Victorious Warrior in their midst (Zephaniah 3:17).

5. The enemy comes to steal, kill, and destroy, but Jesus comes to give life more abundantly (John 10:10).

6. They may feel a new excitement to pray confidently for family members or friends in Jesus name. They have a new experiential Godly testimony.

Don't be surprised if these spiritual encounters happen during church ministry when praying for visitors and members, at community outreaches, street ministry, local or international mission trips, or at any non-church public or private event.

Remember, wherever you go, the Kingdom of Heaven is within you. You bring His Kingdom with you and Jesus' presence radiates through and around you. When I go to a party, an event, or someone's house to minister, I whisper out, "I proclaim the Kingdom of Heaven and God's rule and reign to manifest in this place, in Jesus name." It's also important to expect something to happen. Have on the full armor of God (Ephesians 6:10-18). Be sanctified to the Lord and put up your spiritual antenna and be aware, be ready.

Wherever I go I know the Holy Spirit is at work convicting hearts. A good example is when someone you don't know, apologizes for cursing or being vulgar in your presence. Sometimes they tell you a secret of their heart and they can't believe they just told you, a complete stranger, something they've never told anyone. And amazingly, they feel much better now. This may open an opportunity to lead them to the Lord!

When darkness recognizes Christ in you, It may activate Its fear in the person likely causing them to walk away to avoid you. If this happens in a ministry setting, I walk right up to the person and introduce myself and see what happens. Depending on the circumstances I may do the same thing in other types of gatherings. I personally think its fun to see how darkness manifests before Jesus Christ in me. Sometimes I initially know exactly what spirit is afflicting someone and other times I don't. A few times a demon spoke to me through a person saying, "I know you!" (In a creepy demonic voice), as the person ran away trembling. One woman started to act seductively, so I told her to renounce it, she shook her head no and turned around and ran away. If the person does stick around, I use this as an opportunity to introduce them to Jesus and see what the Lord will do.

Remember Jesus is the deliverer and is using you to bring His love, presence, healing, freedom and salvation to those who need Him. He wants to reveal Himself to their heart. The Holy Spirit will give you the words to speak and He'll never give you more than you can handle. Even if at times it may feel like it. There were times in the beginning of my adventures with the Lord when He stretched me to the max! He used these encounters exposing the spiritual world and demons to teach and give me understanding as well build my confidence in His Victorious Power – making me hungry for more!

Many pastors and leaders do not have the time, desire, faith or knowledge to bring healing and freedom to someone who is demonically oppressed or partially possessed. I once heard a pastor ask someone to "stop manifesting" and suggested they leave the church if they continued to do so. Both "churched" and "unchurched" people don't know where to find help. Some resort to various prescription medications or other addictions to cope. While others float from church to church, meeting to meeting receiving sporadic prayer, finding little relief until they get "plugged-in" to an accepting, loving congregation where healing and deliverance is valued.

Okay, now that I've explained one of many ministry scenarios that can create obstacles, I'd like to tell you a story keeping in mind that I love being used by the Lord to set the captives free (Luke 4:18). The Lord moves fast and doesn't waste any time. So, if someone wants to be effective in prayer ministry, they need a teachable spirit and the Lord will teach them. It is especially important to continually ask the Holy Spirit to teach you to pray effectively. This has everything to do with praying the Heavenly Father's heart in every situation.

You will learn and know His heart from His word and from spending intimate time with Him in your prayer closet – the Secret Place. Fall in love and abide in Him. I would encourage anyone interested in learning how to minister in Holy Spirit power to get plugged in to a spirit-filled, praying church. A church where "hands-on" personal ministry is taught, released and valued. The church is a safe place to "practice" and develop ministry skills and confidence to advance the Kingdom of God.

NOTES

_____

_____

_____

_____

_____

_____

_____

_____

_____

_____

_____

_____

_____

_____

_____

CHAPTER 6

SET THE CAPTIVES FREE
(PART 1 OF 2)

In this chapter:
• A Holy Spirit Teaching Adventure

A Holy Spirit Teaching Adventure

The leader of a local church home group called me. He needed help. One of his regular attendees, Tom, had issues that were deeper than he originally thought. He asked me to come to the next meeting and meet Tom afterwards to pray for him. He said Tom was very anxious to meet with us because he was seeing dark shadows moving in his peripheral vision at home and other places. Occasionally, he was also hearing an angry voice in his ear. Prior to our meeting the home group leader mentioned to Tom that he may need some deliverance. This scared him a little because he didn't understand what deliverance meant or how it could help him in his situation.

My wife, Rebecca and I went to the next meeting and met with Tom afterwards. We sat in folding chairs facing each other. Some of his family members and friends were present for moral and prayer support.

From the look on Tom's face, I could tell he was nervous. I told him not to be afraid and the Lord loves him so much and wants to remove this torment from his life. I also explained that I don't typically use the word "deliverance", because it generates a negative connotation making people uncomfortable by being perceived as bad or evil in some way.

People are often offended or insulted at the insinuation that a demon is working in their life and will not allow you to pray or minister to them. The first time I heard a pastor talk about deliverance I thought he was referring to the Warner Brother's movie from 1972.

Instead of saying, "You need deliverance!," I usually say, "The Lord wants to set you free from the darkness and torment that is afflicting you. Knowingly or unknowingly, you may have allowed it to take root somewhere in your life." In personal ministry it is far more acceptable to say, "You need to be set free," rather than say, "You need deliverance" (Isaiah 61:1 and Luke 4:18).

I went on to assure Tom, deliverance is the love of the Father, through Jesus, invading and pushing out any darkness that is spiritually on the surface and replacing it with His love and light. The Lord will do everything if you ask Him to come into all areas of your heart and life, if you allow Him to. Getting free is simple and easy. But the decision to stay free by doing what is right in the eyes of the Lord as you live your life becomes a challenge to many people.

Sins of unforgiveness, harboring resentment, making negative vows (turning into curses) or jealously are a few reasons darkness can gain access into a person's life. Start by asking them if the Lord is bringing anything to mind concerning the issue they want prayer for. They will usually say, "I don't think so." Or they will indicate they are not sure why darkness is revealing itself more and more in their life.

Tom asked, "What's going to happen?" I responded, "I don't know. Let's agree and ask the Father's love to crowd out or push to the surface anything that doesn't belong." At that time, I noticed Tom's teeth began to chatter a little. This confirmed to me the darkness didn't like our conversation and was beginning to manifest and reveal itself or one of its cohorts (buddies).

Sometimes the person you are praying for will feel the dark spirit of fear. They will think it's their own fearful emotion rather than a spirit, and may ask you to stop praying and even want to leave.

Sometimes dark voices speak to the person's thoughts and feelings convincing them that I am the enemy, and they should get away from me. At this point it's necessary to pray and break the power of the spirit of fear in Jesus' name and inform the person that it's a spirit (outside of them). It is not their own emotional feeling. Usually the fearful, dark spirit knows their time is up and they are going to be evicted because of the presence and authority of the Holy Spirit.

Tom continued to manifest so I asked him, "Are you ready for the love of the Heavenly Father to push this stuff out?" He said, "Yes." I asked him to keep looking at my eyes and I said, "Come, Holy Spirit." All of a sudden, his eyes opened up super-wide and he yelled, "Whooooo!," as he flew up, then backwards on his feet. He was then pushed down onto the floor while knocking over furniture. The noise caused some of his friends in the other room to come running. They had never seen anything like it. He landed 20 feet away from his chair on his back with his body violently shaking. He began yelling, "Help me, help me!," in between the sounds of a growling animal. I quickly followed him to the floor.

This spirit was very angry and wanted to grab and choke me. However, Tom's elbows and shoulders were stuck to the floor. The demon was trying with all its might to get off the floor and strangle me, yet at the same time, it acted fearful because of what it saw in the spirit. It was instantly bound to the floor because of the presence of Jesus Christ and the Holy Spirit in and around me.

Sometimes a person's face will contort, and the Lord will reveal through your spiritual eyesight what the enemy looks like or what its purpose is in their life.

I immediately knew the demon had a legal right or hold on Tom because of sin in his life that he may or may not be aware of. Multiple sins can result in multiple demons along with their cohorts (buddies).

Sometimes a person loves their sin and wants to keep it a secret. Unfortunately, they're not aware the spirit world is real or maybe they don't believe it exists, but their secret sin gives the enemy permission to torment them. Sadly, some Christians don't believe it and will even argue that once you are a spirit-filled, born-again Christian, it is impossible to be oppressed or demonized by an evil spirit. Given my years of experience I can say without a doubt that this is not true. We know darkness or demons gain access through sinful behavior, curses, or victimization. Since we all are sinners, no one is immune. In fact, the sin of unforgiveness is one of the primary reasons for demonic affliction and intense manifestations that can lead to many sicknesses.

Sometimes it's necessary to use the gift of discernment, one of nine spiritual gifts (1 Corinthians 12:7-11) you can operate in. Discernment enables you to determine if the issue is physical, emotional, psychological, spiritual or a combination. If the person has gone to a psychologist or psychiatrist and has been diagnosed or labeled and is on prescription medications, you'll need to ask the Holy Spirit for keen discernment to minister.

If the person is experiencing persistent spiritual issues and is willing, I'll ask them to take a medication vacation with their doctor's permission and oversight. This allows them to feel any emotional pain and it enables the spiritual entities to fully manifest and be dealt with rather than remain subdued and hidden. I try to meet with the person a few times to take full advantage of this drug-free time.

The numbing effect of medications hinders people from readily dealing with the deep spiritual issues of unforgiveness, victimization, or sin in their life. They are typically prescribed to help. They're given for coping, even for a lifetime, with whatever is going on rather than promoting wholeness and healing of the deeper root issues. Don't misunderstand, I believe there is a time and a place for medication. But when its only purpose is to mask a spiritual problem or hinder true healing found in Jesus Christ through prayer, then it's definitely an addictive trap with possible harmful side effects.

As Tom continued to growl, I spoke to the manifesting demon: "In the name of Jesus Christ of Nazareth, I command you to only speak and answer the questions that I ask. Nothing more!" I went on to ask, "By what authority are you here?" The demon replied in an angry garbled voice, "He wants me here." This gave me confirmation there was a harbored or secret sin that needed to be dealt with in order for Tom to be set free. I've heard of times when unaware ministers battled for hours with demonic forces that had a legal right to stay. The end result was tired participants.

Let me start by saying, it's not always wise to talk to demons. I do not recommend talking to them because they are liars and can't be trusted. Sometimes they blurt out their names which can describe their work or the sin that gave them permission or legal right to be there. Knowing their name may help us cut to the chase especially if the person's mind is foggy or they are embarrassed to reveal their sin. A better approach is to command a manifesting demon to be silent and release the person to speak to you in Jesus' name. Then you can interview the person by asking a few questions to help reveal any sin that is giving the enemy permission to torment them. They usually know what it is but don't realize how it can control and affect them. If darkness manifests you can ask the person what they are feeling, seeing, hearing or thinking. This may help reveal a possible root cause and help identify what spirit is manifesting.

Sometimes hidden sin is exposed when another believer recognizes the fruit of it and confronts them. Often, just standing in the same room with a Christian believer can cause a demon within someone to manifest. The darkness is fully aware and recognizes the authority, power and light the believer has in Jesus Christ. It makes them uncomfortable enough to cause them to act out or slightly manifest. Unfortunately, if the believer hasn't been taught about this spiritual reality and the spiritual authority they carry as the Lord's vessel, it is easy for them to conclude that for some strange reason the person doesn't like them. Or worse, the Christian believer may call them a 'crazy person' and warn their church friends to stay away instead of recognizing that the person needs ministry. Remember, as believers we're on assignment. Isaiah 61:1 says, "The Spirit of the Sovereign Lord is on me, because the Lord has anointed me to proclaim good news to the poor. He has sent me to bind up the brokenhearted, to proclaim freedom for the captives and release from darkness for the prisoners."

(continues in the next chapter)

CHAPTER 7

KEEN DISCERNMENT IN MINISTRY LEADS TO FREEDOM
(PART 2 OF 2)

In this chapter:
- Stop Demonic Manifestations and Ask What the Person Is Hearing, Seeing, Thinking and Feeling
- Recognizing Different Types of Manifestations
- Address the Issues and Pray Accordingly

Stop Demonic Manifestations and Ask What the Person Is Hearing, Seeing, Thinking and Feeling

As Tom continued lying on the floor I asked him, "What do you hear or see?" While shaking uncontrollably he held up his phone and fearfully cried out, "They're in my phone! They're in my phone!" I asked, "Who is in your phone?" and he responded, "The demons!" So I immediately wondered if Tom was snared in the sin of pornography giving the darkness a legal right to afflict and attach itself to him.

Remember, demons are legalistic. There is a popular saying in ministry circles, "The enemy takes what you (sinfully) give it and keeps what you (prayerfully) don't take back" (through repentance, forgiveness and using your spiritual authority in Christ).

I commanded the darkness to stop manifesting, in Jesus' name, and it stopped. I helped Tom off the floor and asked him to sit in a chair so I could talk with him. I asked him if he was into pornography. He admitted that he struggled with it for a few years. I also asked him what else was he feeling or thinking about when he was on the floor? The first thing that came to his mind was that he hated his stepfather who used to beat him when he was a child. He added that he hated his mother too, because she always took the stepfather's side and wouldn't try to help.

She wouldn't rescue him from the beatings. He went on to say that as he grew older his stepfather told him to move out of the house or he would kill him. When he told his mother she said it was time for him (Tom) to find another place to live.

Tom's real father left when he was only five years old and hasn't contacted him since. He never knew the love of his earthly father. Now as a young man in his mid-thirties he finds himself as a husband and a father with no idea how to truly love or be loved.

Tom's wife was there and sadly she had no idea of the depth of his struggle with pornography. She was also concerned about the increasing verbal abuse she had experienced over the past year and a half.

After hearing the noise and commotion a few more people came to see what was going on. They asked Tom if it was okay if they stayed during the rest of the prayer, because they had never seen demons manifest and wanted to learn how to minister in this way. I told them that I didn't know what else was going to happen, but Tom welcomed them to watch and pray.

Recognizing Different Types of Manifestations

I knelt down in front of Tom sitting in the chair and asked him to look at me. His eyes started to flair getting wide and then normal again. This is usually a sign that the enemy within is coming up to take a look around. Tom then said he felt like he was going to throw up, but he couldn't. I told Tom, "I know you can't because, in Jesus' name, I don't allow these games." Tom reacted by clenching his fist with his arm pulled back and repeatedly said with a loud voice, "I'm going to hit you, Pat!" He began pleading with me saying, "Pat, get away from me. I'm gonna hit you. I don't want to hit you!" I explained to him that he didn't want to hit me. The darkness did, but it's bound and can't touch me.

It's important to understand that an angry person (not a demon), operating out of their FLESH may hit you. That's why it's always wise to spiritually discern what spirit is speaking to you.

Then suddenly he broke out into an exaggerated, almost hysterical laugh. Some of the people watching were smiling until I told them that it was a mocking spirit laughing at us. I spoke to everyone in the room and said, "Watch and see how much authority you have in Christ." Watch how fast the laughing will stop when this spirit is rebuked.

As he was caught up in hysterical laughter and unaware of what I was going to say, I said, "In the name of Jesus Christ of Nazareth, I command you, mocking spirit, to be silent and go directly to Jesus." Instantly, the spirit stopped, and Tom jumped back into his seat as if the darkness was waiting for its next command. Those watching were amazed. I reminded them again about their authority in Christ and that He is the Deliverer who wants to use them to set the captives free.

I knelt in front of Tom and asked him to look into my eyes once again. Without me saying a word the raging demon manifested. Tom lunged at me but didn't get very far. His back and shoulders were stuck to the chair with his fingers gripped tightly around the seat. I explained to those watching that demons are bound in the presence of Christ in you and there's no need to bind them.

In some ministry circles I've noticed that binding spirits in and around a person receiving prayer becomes very redundant but, in my experience, has no ministry effect. If you minister this way, you reveal to the enemy that you don't realize or fully understand the presence and authority you carry in Christ Jesus.

In order to make the demon stop, I commanded it to be silent and not to manifest as I talked with Tom. Immediately It was calm. It's almost impossible to minister to someone when a demon is manifesting. I purposely show no interest in their distractions.

I asked Tom to look at me again as I prayed. "In Jesus' name, I proclaim the blood of Jesus Christ of Nazareth over the eyes and ears of the enemy to prevent them from hearing or seeing this conversation." I went on to have Tom repeat Parts 1 & 2 of the Salvation Prayer found in the Appendix. (Remember, all dark spirits afflicting Tom can't see or hear any of our conversation at this point.)

Address the Issues and Pray Accordingly

After that, we focused on the spirit of addiction and the sin of pornography. He asked the Lord and his wife to forgive him. He repented and renounced everything concerning these issues. We moved on to deal with the sin of unforgiveness concerning his mother, father, stepfather, and himself. He was reluctant to forgive his parents until I reminded him of what the Lord says about forgiveness. In Matthew 6:15 Jesus tells us how to pray and He addresses unforgiveness. He says if you don't forgive others who sin against you, He won't forgive you of your sins. Also, in Romans 12:19, He reminds us that revenge belongs to Him, "Vengeance is Mine; I will repay, says the Lord."

If Tom wanted a better life – living in freedom – he would have to forgive everyone and give the Lord all of the "baggage" from each of these situations. The Lord freely and gladly takes everything that weighs us down. Matthew 11: 28-30 says it best. "Come to me, all you who are weary and burdened, and I will give you rest. Take my yoke upon you and learn from me, for I am gentle and humble in heart, and you will find rest for your souls. For my yoke is easy and my burden is light."

We dealt with everything that was exposed through forgiveness and understanding. Then I asked Tom to stand up. I told those watching and praying to observe how fast the demons and their cohorts were going to leave. Then Tom interrupted me stating that he's concerned about one more thing before we pray. He recently felt that he may have a spirit of addiction concerning alcohol. He said about four months ago he started drinking late at night to relieve work related pressures and to help him sleep. But in the past two months he finds himself drinking at times during the day. He feels guilty about hiding his drinking issues and realizes that it's hard to stop. I told Tom that in my experience usually a spirit of addiction is attached to a person's tongue and taste buds concerning alcohol drinking and cigarette smoking. But it's also important to change and release any habits and temptations leading up to his drinking and give everything to the Lord, seeking Godly counsel if needed. Tom said that he understood and agreed but wanted me to pray for him against any addiction concerning his drinking before we went forward. Since Tom was already standing in front of me, I had Tom ask the Lord to forgive him for his drinking renouncing it in Jesus name. Then I had him open his mouth briefly and I prayed out in authority; In the name of Jesus Christ of Nazareth, I break the power and its work of any spirit of addiction and its cohorts, that has attached to Toms tongue and taste buds. I command you to leave him now and go directly to Jesus Christ for Him to deal with you. I blessed Toms tongue and taste buds and dedicated them to Jesus Christ of Nazareth under His authority. Tom agreed with everything I prayed. (*Remember everything we just prayed concerning the spirit of addiction and it's cohorts was not yet heard, in the spirit realm, because earlier we proclaimed the blood of Jesus over the eyes and ears of darkness concerning Tom. But the darkness' eyes and ears will be opened to see and hear what we prayed shortly.*) Then I stated, in Jesus name, I ask that next time Tom drinks alcohol that it would taste nasty and remind him of this day. I have heard and seen great results praying this prayer concerning alcohol and cigarettes. Twice I heard people poured out their liquor bottle because it tasted nasty as (Turpentine or Kerosene). A few times I heard many packs of cigarettes were thrown away for the same reason. Unfortunately, if the person persists in their past habitual endeavors, the Lord lets them choose their own desires. (Just a point of reference, we have between 2,000-4,000 taste buds, most of them located on the tongue. The sensory cells in the taste buds are renewed once a week).

Now we continued to pray for Tom in agreement where we originally paused. I asked Tom, "Are you ready to be set free? Because you're going to feel some stuff leave." I told him he was going to feel much better and his life was going to change. He smiled and said, "Let's do it!"

I asked him to look at my eyes one last time. I asked the Lord to open the eyes and ears of the (enemy) darkness and its cohorts (that were afflicting him) to hear our prayers of agreement and everything that Tom just confessed, repented, renounced and asked forgiveness for. Suddenly, Tom's eyes opened really wide as the Lord allowed the darkness to hear every word. Tom's shoulders jumped up as the darkness mumbled a few parting words and that was it! Tears rolled down his face and he gave me a big hug. He went around to everyone in the room to thank them for praying. He was saying, "They're gone! They're gone! Thank you, Jesus! They're gone!"

I asked him, "What did he feel?" He said, "It felt like some small stuff and then something big was quickly pulled through him, up and out through his shoulders, leaving him feeling light and free."

We ended by asking the Holy Spirit and the Heavenly Father's love to fill every void where darkness once occupied. We proclaimed the blood of Jesus over any spiritual open doors that had access to Tom in the spirit. We warned Tom about increased temptation since the darkness was angry about losing its territory. We anointed his phone, broke the power of anything of darkness that traveled through it and dedicated it to the Lord. We suggested that he stop using his phone and any other devices connected to the Internet until he could arrange for ongoing counseling with a church or ministry that would help keep him accountable. This would help bring healing to him and his family.

I heard that Tom had taken a new job in another state a few months later and I've not heard from him since.

NOTES

CHAPTER 8

DIVINE APPOINTMENTS

In this chapter:
- Be Ready for the Unexpected With the Lord
- Being a Vessel of The Lords Manifest Love

Be Ready for the Unexpected With the Lord

An important lesson I learned early on is to not touch a person who is manifesting a demon (darkness) and not let them touch me. If you attempt to grab or hold the person's arm, they will want to arm-wrestle you or start pushing and pulling you. Sometimes they may even try to bite you which you obviously don't want to happen. Don't be afraid of a person who is manifesting darkness, just use wisdom. The darkness is terrified seeing Jesus Christ in and around you, so always be conscious of that. Remember, Jesus is the Deliverer, not you. The Holy Spirit will tell you what to do or say. He is our Teacher and Comforter.

I've had many encounters with people manifesting a demon who wanted to physically engage me. The following is just one of many experiences:

While I was praying for a few people after a meeting, a man came to me and asked if I would pray for him. I said, "Sure." I stood in front of him as I asked, "What do you want prayer for?" I was staring at his eyes as I waited for his response. Eventually he started to breathe heavy and then he loudly cursed a couple of words at me and suddenly began to manifest an angry, raging demon. He stood in front of me, toe-to-toe with his chest lightly bumping mine in an attempt to provoke me. The demon continued to curse me in a loud voice. All the while, the man was holding his arms down at his side with his fists tightly clenched. He was poised and ready to fight. He stood with his nose a few inches from mine in a threatening manner. In response, while holding my arms and hands down and behind me out of his reach, I stood with my chest out against his to keep his face further away from mine. I continued to stare into the man's intense, flaring, manifesting eyes. Then I spoke, "I rebuke and break your power in Jesus' name." I usually keep a straight face but sometimes I smile at them which sometimes really amps up the demonic rage.

Suddenly the man (demon) let out a very long, angry, resisting grunt as if the Lord put His hand on top of his head and pushed him down to the floor on his knees in front of me (Christ in me). Remember we can do nothing of ourselves. Jesus is the victorious warrior in our midst and the battle belongs to the Lord. (2 Chronicles 20:15) We are betrothed to be His bride, He is intensely in love with us and He will not let the enemy hurt us. Remember He already defeated the enemy at the cross.

At this point, I knelt down in front of the man as he was still manifesting the angry demon, but he was now more subdued. I stared into his eyes and said, "I rebuke and command you to release him in Jesus' name." I continued to look into his eyes and said to the man, (not the demon), "Yes, your Heavenly Father loves you," repeating it over and over. Eventually his lips started quivering as he loudly sobbed and fell forward leaning on me with his head on my left shoulder, repeatedly saying, "I'm sorry. Forgive me. Forgive me." The deep sobbing intensified as I placed my arms around him to prevent him from falling over. Moments later his body and arms went limp and he appeared to let go and surrender. I believe the Lord set him free of the manifesting demon as he cried out, "Forgive me." I did not discern any presence of darkness on him anymore.

Being a Vessel of the Lord's Manifest Love

I held him even tighter so he wouldn't' slip away and fall. As the crying slowed down, I could feel that my left shoulder was soaked with his tears. I became uncomfortable kneeling and holding him and wanted to lay him down because I couldn't hold him any longer. But right before I was about to lay him down, I clearly heard the Lord say, "You're not holding him, I AM." Moments later I caught the revelation of what the Lord spoke which made me almost cry. However, knowing that the Lord was holding him, through me, gave me enough strength to hang on for a little while longer.

The man was still kneeling, but suddenly sat back on his heels and looked a little startled because of what just happened. He apologized again and said that he now felt very light. I asked, "What has happened to make you so upset?" He went on to explain that His wife and son moved out about a year ago, but he still loved his wife. Unfortunately, a few months ago, he found out that she had a boyfriend. And this week he was served divorce papers, the final blow.

We talked a while longer and he told me he forgave his wife while crying on my shoulder. I asked him, "Why do you think she left?" He told me most of the problems started after he joined a new band about a year ago. The band only practiced a few hours a week and played together for an hour another day. Of course, he also practiced the songs at home for a few months during that time. He didn't think his wife would mind, but he was wrong. It was not long before his wife didn't like the band, their songs or his new friends. Eventually, she didn't like being around him either. He went on to say that he couldn't understand or resolve all the issues that upset her.

As he was leaving, I asked him what kind of band he was in? He responded by saying, "I play guitar and sing at times in a church band." I asked him, "Are you saying that it's a church worship team band?" And he said, "Yes, it was a new church that we started to attend as a family more than a year ago.

Many times the enemy is the culprit and very crafty in destroying the marriages of Christian families through the hidden deceptive workings of the Spirit of division, which I discuss in the next chapter

NOTES

CHAPTER 9

THE SPIRIT OF DIVISION

In this chapter:
- Its Secret Ability to Divide and Destroy Marriages
- Prayer Ministry That Teaches Couples

Its Secret Ability to Divide and Destroy Marriages

The spirit of division may be one prevailing reason behind Christian separation and divorce. The enemy knows that a house divided against itself cannot stand (Mark 3:25). It intentionally targets individuals, families, and church leaders who are hungry and praying for the manifest presence of God. The spirit of division and its work are not often mentioned, revealed or taught in churches today.

The enemy can attach itself to a person's unhealed emotional hurts, past traumas, victimization. Then It can undetectably influence or activate irrational emotions in a person's life. Unconfessed sin can allow darkness to be present in a person for an entire lifetime. A few additional examples can be negative vows, judgments, jealousy, anger, fear, unbelief, witchcraft, curses, and occult practices

If a person or family never went to church or has attended a "spiritually dead" church for years where leaders and programs are lifted up, then decides to go to a more "alive" church where Jesus Christ and the Holy Spirit are valued, expected, and lifted up, they may unknowingly encounter spiritual warfare. I can almost guarantee that in a short time a person with an unknown attachment to spiritual darkness may begin to manifest because of the exposing light of Jesus Christ's presence in the new church they started to attend (John 8:12). Now the enemy does not want Its hidden place of attachment on a person exposed by the light of Jesus. It will feel threatened in a church with an atmosphere filled with the Holy Spirit light. So, the enemy may manifest a covert secret attack or distraction to prevent their exposure in the light. Darkness wants to get away from the heavy presence of the Holy Spirit. To prevent the new family from attending the spirit filled church sometimes the darkness will use any open spiritual doors to interrupt or stop their attendance. The enemy usually stirs up and orchestrates unforeseen relational problems at home between the spouses. This spiritual battle ground is not exposed in depth in the churches, so the naive unsuspecting spouses are unprepared and blind sighted to the invisible spiritual warfare initiating relational attacks. It's important for Christians to learn and understand their spiritual weapons and protection that can be put on spiritually every day to protect them from the enemy schemes and attacks (Ephesians 6:10-18).

All the enemy or the accuser of the brethren has to do to stir up trouble is whisper lies in a wife or husband's ear (negative personal thoughts). This often activates past unhealed negative feelings, hurts, trauma and emotions. They begin to blame their spouse for an array of past or present resolved or unresolved issues. This leaves one spouse feeling like a victim of untrue hurtful verbal accusations while the other may feel rejected, angered, without a real clue of what is going on, or why their spouse is in denial of the accusations. The enemy continues Its work to develop an arsenal of misunderstandings, confusion, accusations, and blame between them. It's all designed to bring division and ultimately can negatively affect the marriage. This can cause a distraction when going to church or split the spouses by keeping them from attending church together. Possibly in time the enemy may be the culprit stopping both spouses from attending a spirit-filled church service.

One spouse may have more negative spiritual baggage than the other. The Holy Spirit's light is brighter in the spouse that has less or no baggage. Darkness will not like the light emanating from the other spouse and will not want it to increase through the new church fellowship. It will do whatever it can to get away from the light of Christ.

As a person begins to grow in faith, learning how to love and be loved by their Heavenly Father and understand their authority in Jesus, the Holy Spirit's presence begins to emanate brighter through them, exposing the darkness. When two people come into agreement in spiritual prayer, in this case, husband and wife, their prayers are 10 times more powerful then praying alone. The enemy is aware of this powerful truth. So, if the couple starts to practice praying together, becoming a powerful weapon in the spirit, the enemy will try to divide and conquer their effectiveness. As a person realizes their spiritual authority in Christ, the enemy knows he can soon be cast out. It's important that all sins are confessed, and the blood of Jesus covers all open doors in the spirit concerning both spouses and they have wise counsel available. Many families are not aware of the enemy's schemes causing spousal division. When families learn the enemy's tactics they become a pillar of strength in Christ that will not easily be moved.

When I pray with couples in similar situations typically one spouse is reacting against the other because of a combination of one or all of the following influences:

1. They believe a lie that the enemy (accuser) whispered in their ear about their spouse that dredged up past issues.

   · The enemy's lies and accusations typically focus on what has been wrongfully said or done in the past or even the present. It always takes advantage of an opportunity to distort the present or reignite the past. The enemy vindictively doses the situation with fuel and lights it with a match turning it into a forest fire of destructive emotions.

2. They react to the situation without realizing they are manifesting emotions that aren't their own. These emotions usually belong to the manifesting spirit (darkness). It could be a dark spirit that is attached to one or more of the person's emotions that was not healed from a former trauma or sin. It's a coordinated deceptive spiritual attack that is felt or realized in the natural as darkness continually speaks negatively in their ears from the spirit world, while simultaneously triggering Its attached negative emotion. People are totally unaware of Its spiritual-natural manifesting effective capabilities.

   · 2 Timothy 1:7 tells us, "For God has not given us a spirit of fear, but of power and of love and of a sound mind." On many occasions I renounced a spirit of fear and it left the person. Fear can be an intense emotion, a feeling that seems like it's our own, but it's not! (Hmm… bet you never thought about that did you?)

   · John 8:44 says the devil "…is a liar and the father of lies." So, it only makes sense that a dark spirit would be a liar, too. If a spirit of fear, rejection, anger, rage, or abandonment manifests, it may be the enemy's attempt to trick a person into believing their reaction or feeling is the result of their human emotions from the past or the present rather than the falsely triggered emotions of darkness.

3. They stuffed to their lower belly past unhealed hurts, disappointments, broken promises, or rejection that triggered current emotions to manifest. I will talk more about this later.

It takes a discerning minister or a discerning family member to identify and expose this type of demonic attack or spiritual warfare against a marriage covenant. Once it is identified and understood it's easy for a couple to be free of the enemy's divisive tactics and understand that the battle isn't against each other but against the darkness (Ephesians 6:12).

Returning to the story of the young family attending the new church where the husband joined the worship team, I believe the enemy orchestrated all of the couple's reactions simultaneously to cause division and end their marriage. Unfortunately, I only had a chance to minister to the husband. I truly believe the issues in their marriage were motivated by the enemy's dark forces.

In counseling situations, you'll begin to discuss issues in detail and recognize that one spouse or the other is obviously confused about why and what they are feeling and unable to hold onto the truth concerning the issues. This is a good indicator that the enemy may be at work. Because of this deception, the manifesting spouse usually has no idea why or what caused the sudden reaction and accusatory blow-up.

Usually they are responding to a feeling that actually has no true basis for being there. Remember, the enemy comes to steal, kill and destroy (John 10:10-12). The enemy and his cohorts use this situation to laugh at you as it brings division and destroys your marriage. This, in turn, hurts your children and your entire family. Remember, the battle is not between flesh and blood (Ephesians 6:12-18).

Prayer Ministry that Teaches Couples:

1. Recognize and defeat the enemy's work by praying together in agreement (Matthew 18:19-20).

2. A) Pray with authority and command the darkness to stop its work and be silent. B) Plead the blood of Jesus over all the plans and games the enemy's tactics. C) Command all the enemy's plans in your life and marriage to be null and void in Jesus name.

3. Deal with (not avoid) past issues that resurface and cause torment by continually releasing forgiveness to each other.

4. Proclaim the blood of Jesus Christ over each others ears. The enemy cannot speak through the blood. The enemy cannot get through the blood of Jesus Christ to them. Once this is done a battle in your mind still remains – the lingering, untrue, negative words that were spoken. These are the words and thoughts that were planted previously by the enemy or by each other. Break the power of all negative words and curses in Jesus name.

Release their mind from this torment by recognizing that they were played by a lying, deceitful spirit. Release the negative thoughts and move on! If this solution doesn't work, then bring all remaining negative thoughts captive to the mind of Christ (2 Corinthians 10:5).

5. Put on the full armor of God every morning and be spiritually alert, be aware (Ephesians 6:10-18). They can also proclaim Psalm 91 over themselves and family for protection.

6. Seek wise counsel.

7. *This is optional but very effective.* Play worship music 24-hours a day in your house. Set the volume low enough so you can't hear it or as loud as you like. Pray and ask the Lord to turn up or blast the volume in the spirit realm. The worship music fills your home with the presence of the Holy Spirit and drives out any dark spirits that are hanging around. I suggest you bless and dedicate the radio to Jesus Christ of Nazareth. Anoint the volume and station buttons including the power cord and plug. This will stop the enemy from tampering with it. This may sound excessive, but its not. In all my years of ministry, I've witnessed how darkness can turn down the volume, change the channel and even unplug and knock the radio or device to the floor. But that's another story.

It is a lot easier to win a battle when you are aware of who the enemy is and understand its tactics. You want to know it's tactics, it's games and it's purpose. You want to know where the arrows are coming from and why. It is written that we are more than conquerors in Christ Jesus (Romans 8:37-39).

We encourage couples to stand and fight together as one. As they use the spiritual weapons given to them, they will start to believe the truth, and become overcomer's in Christ. They will start to realize as they stand and fight together the Lord does the battle on their behalf. "Resist the devil and he will flee from you" (James 4:7).

You become an effective part of the Army of God as you learn, understand, and catch your Heavenly Father's loving heart for you (Ephesians 6:13). You'll experience His authority. You'll know His presence because He lives inside you. The spiritual world will open up to you. The enemy will tremble and run as you continue to minister and teach others to walk in His presence, love, power, and light. Learning to set the captives free through Jesus Christ is exciting. You'll see lives change for the better, remarkably, right in front of you.

NOTES

CHAPTER 10

HEALING "STUFFED" HURTS: DISAPPOINTMENT, BROKEN PROMISES, REJECTION AND MORE

In this chapter:
* Understanding Hidden Stuffed Emotions
* Releasing Stuffed Emotions

Understanding Hidden Stuffed Emotions

In an effort to be strong, we "suck-it up," hiding our pain to survive. It allows us to move forward in our lives. People often stuff their hurts, traumas, disappointments, broken promises, and issues of victimization. They stuff them down into the pit of their lower belly without realizing it. What they also don't realize is that spiritual darkness can attach itself to the emotional hurt or whatever is being stuffed. Darkness can attach itself to those emotions, unhealed wounds and repressed anger. This puts the enemy in a position to deceitfully play with a person's feelings by manipulating those stuffed emotions from the hurts or traumas that they experienced in the past. The enemy can spiritually speak thoughts into a person's ears causing emotions to activate or be triggered with very little apparent recognition or reasons.

The person feels sick and anxious concerning their emotions, and they are unable to identify the cause. But see, the enemy has attached itself to their lingering hurts in their hidden stuffed emotions. The deceitful enemy plays games and manifests itself in those stuffed, negative emotions. No wonder the person is unable to decipher the cause.

In fact, this is in part how multiple personalities and disassociation may begin. I will explain fully how and why multiple personalities take root and how Jesus easily sets them free in another informative book I'm writing. I also cover freedom from recurring nightmares which is useful in past trauma experiences and in P.T.S.D. Remember, Jesus came to set the captives free! He brings healing to hidden spiritual issues and wholeness to our souls.

All of this can result in various illnesses. A few common physical symptoms that can occur over time are ulcers, acid reflux, and other digestive problems. When I minister to someone with these issues I start by placing their hand on their lower belly with my hand on top of theirs and say:

Releasing Stuffed Emotions

"In the name of Jesus Christ of Nazareth, I bless and release the love of the Abba Father to the pit of your belly. In Jesus name, I break the power of all darkness and its cohorts that are attached to your emotions (including but not limited to): broken promises, disappointments, vows, abandonment, fear (or whatever the Holy Spirit brings to mind) that you stuffed down in your belly to be strong. I dedicate and bless your entire lower belly and all of your emotions to Jesus Christ of Nazareth. I proclaim and release the presence and consuming fire and light of Jesus Christ to consume all darkness even in hidden areas of emotions. I command all darkness and shadows attached to all emotions or anywhere else in the belly to come into the light of Jesus Christ. Right now, in Jesus' name!

Then I release and speak freedom to all of the emotions. I usually ask if they are feeling anything and minister accordingly as the Holy Spirit leads. As you are praying don't be surprised if someone's belly reacts to the presence of the Lord by quickly moving in and out. I ask the Lord to push out any darkness with His love and replace it with His presence. He's the healer and sets them free right away. I would advise you to have other prayer warriors come into agreement with the prayers being prayed if that is possible.

Several people who received this type of prayer said they had a disgusting bowel movement within a day after the prayer ministry. But they all felt great afterwards and all their stomach issues were gone. I tell them to thank the Lord for their emotional or physical healing.

CHAPTER 11

WITCHCRAFT – ONE OF MANY TRUE STORIES
(PART 1 OF 2)

In this chapter:
- Darkness Manifests in the Presence of the Lord in YOU!
- Ask Questions and Spiritually Discern

My friend Phil called and asked if I could pray for his coworker's sick mother one night. He worked with a lady named Jane. We made the appointment for the following week. I met Phil at his house and we drove to Jane's house together. I prayed for Phil a year earlier and he received the Lord as his Savior and experienced a light touch from the Holy Spirit. Unfortunately, he never pursued the Lord. I did tell him many Holy Spirit stories, though, and he told some of them to his coworkers. This is why Jane wanted prayer for her bed-ridden mother.

Darkness Manifests in the Presence of the Lord in YOU!

As we walked into Jane's house she greeted us and invited us into her dining room to talk a little. She wanted to know what religion I was involved in. Jane was raised Catholic although she lives a free lifestyle. The three of us sat there in her dining room as I proceeded to tell her that I was raised Catholic as a child and attended four years of Catholic elementary school. I mentioned that I now attend a non-denominational, spirit-filled church where praying for and ministering to people through the power of the Holy Spirit is taught and highly valued. All of a sudden she apologized and said, "I don't want to be rude, but for some reason it bothers me to look at you." I said, "That's OK you don't have to apologize," realizing that some kind of darkness is starting to manifest. Then her teeth started chattering a little and she covered them with her hand. In a few moments her teeth started chattering uncontrollably. Then she said that for some reason she felt very cold. At that point I knew that an occult spirit was beginning to manifest. She was also embarrassed because her face was flushed. I quickly looked over at my friend Phil and he just rolled his eyes at me. He obviously didn't catch that a demonic manifestation was going on right in front of him.

When I looked back at Jane, she now had both hands over her mouth and was trying to stop her teeth from chattering. She said, "Oh my God! This is really weird. This never happened before." I was concerned that she was going to ask us to leave. I quickly asked her if she ever used a Ouija board when she was younger? She said, "No." Then I asked her if she was ever involved or participated in witchcraft or rituals and again, she said, "No." Since she wasn't looking at me, I whispered under my breath and commanded all dark spirits that were manifesting to be still, in Jesus' name. And almost immediately her teeth stopped chattering.

She took her hand away from her mouth and said, "Wow, that was strange. Where did that come from?" Jane had no idea that she was manifesting darkness and didn't seem to pay attention to my probing questions about witchcraft. At this point, I continued to ask her if she ever participated in a séance or made any blood vows? She replied, "No!" And then, I offered to pray a blessing over her before we pray for her mother. She agreed and said she would like that. I thought this would also give me the opportunity to pray for her to see what the Lord was going to do to set her free.

It was obvious that she had no idea the dark presence that was around her and attached to her. The darkness could have been there for years hiding, but the presence and light of Jesus Christ exposed it. I asked her to stand up and look at me. I also asked for her permission to put my hand on her head to pray and ask the Holy Spirit to come upon her. She said, "Sure, no problem."

As I placed my hand on her head, all that I was able to say was "Come, Holy Spirit." Suddenly her head started shaking erratically back and forth, really fast, as her nose went over her shoulders in each direction. I stood there and watched as her hair was whipping back and forth across her face. I looked over at my wide-eyed friend who was sitting down saying quietly, "Oh boy, I don't like this." I just smiled at him and then looked back at Jane.

Ask Questions and Spiritually Discern

She suddenly stopped shaking her head and stood there with her head down and her eyes closed with her chin resting on her chest for a while. The head-shaking episode lasted about 30 seconds. She suddenly took one big gasp of air as she quickly picked her head up. She said, "O my God, I thought that I was going to throw up for a second." I asked, "What did you see or hear?" She said that she didn't hear anything, so I asked her again if she saw anything. She went on to tell me that all she saw was darkness, heavy black darkness, and then in an instant a beautiful rainbow appeared and before it was completely formed the top section broke off and fell to the ground. After this happened she was able to pick up her head and come out of that place or vision.

The Lord confirmed to me that the rainbow represented His covenant with her and that it was broken because of something sinful she had done. I asked her again if she was ever involved in any darkness like witchcraft or tarot cards. She responded with an assertive, "No!" I went on to tell her a Bible story where the Lord made a covenant with Noah that He would never flood the earth again and the sign of His promise (covenant) was a rainbow (Genesis 9:16). I said I knew the Lord was going to do something for her after seeing her reaction from putting my hand on her head and praying a few words. She thought I had my hands on both sides of her head and that I was twisting her head back and forth very fast. She said she couldn't understand why I was doing that. I explained that I couldn't make her head move back and forth that fast and that I only had my hand on the top of her head for a few seconds.

Phil spoke up and confirmed what I said. She still didn't believe me, so I told her to sit in the chair while I knelt down on one knee in front of her at a distance almost out of her reach. I asked her to look at my eyes as I slowly reached over and touched her knee with one finger. Instantly, her eyes immediately rolled back in her head and her head began to radically shake back and forth again as her hair whipped across her face. It continued for about 20 seconds this time. And again, it abruptly stopped with her chin resting on her chest as if she were asleep. Phil and I waited as we watched her. This time (in approximately 10 seconds) with a big gasp for air she lifted her head and released a burping, dry heave while she covered her mouth. Again, she thought she was going to throw up.

I moved close in front of her and asked her to look at my eyes. I wanted to see if anything was going to manifest. Then I asked her again if she saw anything. She was a little shook up and said, "Everything was pitch black and I was standing in this creepy darkness when in an instant a very distinct large face of a white cat appeared right in front of my face and was staring at me which was very weird."

At that point I said I didn't care what she told me, but that I knew at some point in her life she was involved in white magic and possibly other dark practices. Please note: Don't' be deceived. The source is the same for both white and black magic – the devil.

Before I continue this story (in the next chapter), let me explain a few things.

After attending my church ministry training class where I was being "trained-up". I began to see all kinds of demonic manifestations. Demons were often manifesting in church ministry as well as in everyday situations. One time early in my adventures with the Lord, I saw a demon's scary-looking face on another person who was looking at me. It freaked me out and caused my heart to race. Another time an angry demon cursed at me using a man's voice coming out of a woman's mouth.

Years ago, before I asked the Lord to teach me and use me to set the captives free, I never imagined the spiritual world was so real. I definitely did not believe that demons existed in today's world. I obviously was very naive and deceived especially concerning their effect on people's lives today.

I told my pastor about these experiences and that they made me feel afraid at times. He strongly admonished me, saying, "Don't ever, ever be afraid of darkness manifesting. You don't cause them to manifest. The presence of the Lord in you does. And He is going to use you to help set the captives free! You are not the Deliverer. He is. He knows exactly what He's doing and is going to do. So don't ever worry about a thing, He will protect you. He will give you wisdom and will lead you in what to do and say. Just abide in Him" (2 Samuel 22:3-7). He told me, "The manifesting demons won't be able to touch you because they are bound by the presence of the Lord within you and around you. But the person's flesh can hit you." Sometimes, a person, in their anger, can sound like a demon while experiencing their emotional pain. The spiritual gift of discernment will clarify the situation.

I took his words to heart and since then I always feel disconnected from fear of any instant demonic manifestations that occurs during ministry. I've come to realize that the Lord is exposing It and I know in a short amount of time that the manifesting darkness will be history, resulting in another cool Holy Spirit testimony. Remember, the Lord is no respecter of people. He will use any of His children the same way if you make yourself available.

Practice makes you realize that He is perfect every time and what moves Him is love. One of the things that makes Him smile at you is your obedience to Him. He hates the darkness and sets the captives free. The only superstar during ministry is the Lord Jesus and the Holy Spirit. Our Heavenly Father joyously celebrates as ONE in His Son and the Holy Spirit. His children are being set free from the devil's grip and being prepared to come home to Him. They are becoming ONE in Jesus and together becoming ONE in Him (John 17:21).

(continues in the next chapter)

CHAPTER 12

JESUS RELEASES JANE FROM SPIRITUAL CAPTIVITY

(PART 2 OF 2)

In this chapter:
- Abide in the Lord and Ask Questions
- Five Simple Steps to Deliverance
- Spiritually Discern and Trust in the Lord
- Ministry Strategies and Being a Vessel of His Love

I could have prayed to break the power of the manifestations that were causing Jane's head to shake back and forth, but I knew it would have delayed finding out the root cause. I felt the Lord's peace to let the head shaking continue and see how it played out.

Abide in the Lord and Ask Questions

Jane already told me that she didn't remember being involved in any witchcraft, but the manifestations were telling me otherwise, so I continued asking her questions. It's very important to ask the person you're praying for what they see, hear, and feel during the ministry time. Typically, they only tell you specifically about what you ask them and nothing more. Asking questions helps cut to the chase of why, when, and where the dark spirit gained access to the person, otherwise known as "the enemy's hook". Again, remember that it is easy for a person to be set free (delivered). The Lord sets the captives free. Pastors and ministers of the Lord may use other strategies of prayer for releasing the captives as the Lord leads. What I have written is my truthful experience and what I have been taught by the Lord. It has been very successful and quick. I continue to learn as the Lord continues to give me divine appointments and teaches me. My desire is to be obedient to Him. I pray that my heart stays humble before Him so my flesh doesn't impede or get in the way and delay deliverance. I truly want people set free and delivered as His divine, teaching appointments continue in my life.

Five Simple Steps to Deliverance

Recognize the sin or issues that needs to be confessed before the Lord. I always look to identify the root causes by continually discerning as I listen to the person's story. The root cause can also be acquired by simple knowledge, revelation, or counseling.

1. Confess out loud the sin that gave the darkness access.

2. Repent. Ask the Lord for forgiveness.

3. Renounce the sin and any attached darkness and command it to leave and not return, in Jesus name.

4. Ask the Holy Spirit to fill any vacant place that the darkness once occupied with the perfect love of the Abba Father. His love will crowd out any lingering residue of darkness.

5. Go and sin no more.

Please note there may be spiritual resistance or manifestations within these steps. Keep moving forward.

That's usually the extent of it. The Holy Spirit may lead you to deeper issues at any point, so follow His leading.

Jane's vision of the rainbow revealed that a covenant with the Lord had been broken and that she was involved in some sort of witchcraft that she couldn't remember. So, we said a quick prayer and asked the Lord to bring to her memory any time that she participated in witchcraft or anything else where access was given.

I sat facing Jane while we waited for the Lord to reveal the point of access. Suddenly, her eyes flared with fear and confusion as she looked at me. I immediately discerned that the enemy put a mask of deception in front of my face to convince Jane that I was the enemy and to get away from me. When I explained to Jane what was happening she didn't react at all. This seemed odd, so I asked her if she could hear me. She continued to look at me with a strange expression on her face without saying a word. At this point I realized and discerned that the enemy had deafened her ears so she couldn't hear me.

I pointed at her and said, "In Jesus' name, I break the power of the deaf and dumb spirit on you right now." I asked her again if she could hear me and this time she responded, "Yes, I can." I told her once again that the enemy was putting a deceptive mask in front of my face. The enemy was trying to fearfully convince her that I was the enemy. Darkness was attempting to scare her into stopping the ministry and telling us to leave. She acted surprised and told me that was exactly what she was thinking and feeling. She said that it looks like I have a tan stocking over my face only showing eye sockets and an impression of my nose and mouth.

I asked her to point at my face and rebuke all spirits of deception in Jesus name. She just sat there. So, I asked her again if she could hear me. After no response, I realized that the enemy had deafened her ears again! So again, I broke the power of the deaf and dumb spirit and commanded it to leave her in Jesus' name. After this, Jane looked at me and said, "What?" I immediately proclaimed the blood of Jesus over her ears so that the enemy couldn't make her deaf again. Once again, I told her to point at my face and break the power of the spirit of deception in Jesus' name. As soon as she finished speaking the command her whole body jumped as if she got an electrical shock. She said, "What was that?" Then she told me that my face looked normal again. Obviously, the darkness was concerned that it was going to be evicted and was doing its best to hold the ground it acquired many years ago.

Spiritually Discern and Trust in the Lord

Suddenly, Jane remembered something. Now in her late 40's, she remembered being 17 and going to a friend's house for a séance to call up the spirit of Joan of Arc. (*It wasn't the first time I encountered this same issue.*) She recalled that her friend who was leading the séance was really into the dark side. She said, "As we stood in a circle holding hands, my friend rattled off some words requesting that Joan of Arc's spirit come forth. After a few minutes I felt like I was on fire and as if I was actually burning at the stake. I screamed and ran into her bathroom and jumped into her shower fully dressed and quickly turned on the water using both hands turning both knobs on full blast! At first it didn't feel like it was working which really scared me. Then suddenly I began to cool off and get some relief. My friend, who was leading the séance came in the bathroom and started laughing at me. She and the others thought I was joking as I stood in her shower, soaking wet!"

Jane went on to say that the real joke was that her friend wanted to continue and call up other dead people's spirits from hundreds of years ago. She said, "I told her what I felt was real. I told her she was nuts. I told everyone there, 'I'm out of here!,' and went home to change out of my wet clothes."

At this point, I asked Jane why didn't she mention this story before? She assured me, in all honesty, that she didn't remember what happened until after we prayed and asked the Lord to bring back any memories needed for healing. This memory popped up in her mind right after that prayer.

This is why it's important to pray and ask the Lord to reveal why a demonic manifestation occurred. It is important to discern what spirit it is and how it got access especially when the person doesn't recall. Of course, there may be other issues that pop up as the Lord deals with the demonic presence on the surface. *Keep in mind that she also may have been involved in other issues.* Remember, the Lord is our pilot and we are His Copilot. Always allow Him to direct the course of the ministry. The Lord can dig deep into a person's heart exposing forgotten tragedies, deep secrets and forgotten negative vows. He wants His children free and healed.

I asked Jane to stand up as we prayed for the Holy Spirit to move on her behalf. Then we led Jane through the five steps to deliverance/release mentioned earlier. She experienced some resistance, but we continued to pray. *Remember: keep your eyes on the Lord and not the enemy during ministry.* When she renounced the enemy and commanded it to leave her in Jesus' name, her body suddenly and yet very slowly began twisting back and forth as she was raising herself up on her toes. Her neck appeared to be stretched with her chin being pulled upward toward the ceiling. It looked like the Lord was pulling the dark spirit off of her from the ground up which is likely opposite of the way it came upon her.

It reminded me of when I was five or six years old. My mother would have me put my arms straight up in the air as she pulled my t-shirt off. The small neck opening always got stuck around my neck under my chin which only made my mother pull harder causing me to raise up on my toes with the shirt still tugging up under my chin. It eventually slid up over my face while almost taking my ears off with one last aggressive pull. And then I was free of it.

As I watched Jane being stretched to the max, I looked down to make sure her toes were still touching the floor. Suddenly the dark spirit was completely pulled off her, as if it was an attached curse and she was released. Very cool! We prayed and asked the Holy Spirit to fill and consume any empty voids remaining within her with the Abba Father's love. She began to tremble as the love of God started filling and occupying all empty areas within her. After a few minutes she said she felt really good.

The three of us, our friend Phil, Jane, and I, experienced the Lord setting a captive free! Jane felt wiped out after the ordeal and we didn't get a chance to pray for Jane's mother which was the main reason that Phil and I went over there. I guess the Lord had other plans.

There are so many other experiences that flood my mind that are great teaching true stories as the Lord involved me in His endeavors. I want to reveal some understanding or valuable ministry techniques during some demonic challenging manifestations.

Ministry Strategies and Being a Vessel of His Love

At times you may encounter darkness that is verbally manifesting, stating its high-ranking name or position displaying a bully and controlling attitude. It may have a few hidden cohorts of lesser rank in its presence for supportive encouragement or help if needed. Remember darkness is darkness no matter who it says it is. Jesus defeated all of them at the cross, so don't be intimidated, keep your eyes on the Lord. The confrontation is the Lords', and you are His vessel being used to set the captive free.

The Lord showed me once how to separate a dark, rebellious, bully spirit from dark spirits of hierarchy and its present cohorts – which accelerated the person's freedom. The Lord told me to command the manifesting darkness to look at my eyes. Then, in Jesus' name, I commanded all dark spirits of hierarchy and it's present cohorts to be silent and not communicate with each other - including the dark rebellious bully spirit. I broke the power of their communication and proclaimed the blood of Jesus over all their words. I then proclaimed the blood of Jesus above, below and on both sides of this dark, commanding, bully spirit singling it out by itself so it can't hear or see anything in Jesus' name.

Wow, what an attitude change. It began trembling profusely in fear calling out to lucifer/satan for help... saying, "You promised you'd help me!" I broke the power of this request and commanded it to fall to the ground powerless in Jesus' name. I commanded the spirit to leave, stating that this person is not its home anymore because their sins are forgiven and you have no more authority/spiritual legal rights concerning them. I then commanded it to go directly to Jesus Christ for Him to deal with, in Jesus' name. It left immediately and I observed that its cohorts were removed also.

This also works really well when dealing with a demonic strongman in charge of a few cohorts who are working together in an area of a persons life. (Sometimes it's also effective when working with multiple personalities.) As the strongman gets cast out, one to three cohorts under its command also get expelled at the same time.

I tested the deliverance by commanding the dark bully spirit to come up to make sure it left in Jesus' name. There was no response. The person it was secretly attached to or tormenting usually senses or feels its absence. In other instances, it's good to test its absence (if you discern to do so) because it may remain hidden due to a ministry misunderstanding or by mispronouncing its name. Mispronouncing its unusual demonic name may legally/spiritually give it permission to stay. On occasion, I have commanded dark spirits with strange demonic names to speak its name very slowly, even syllable by syllable, in Jesus name. Then I immediately speak its name back correctly (syllable by syllable) breaking its power and work commanding it to leave in Jesus name. Totally Amazing! After the release, I ask the Holy Spirit to fill all spiritual voids with the Heavenly Fathers Love, in the name of Jesus. Sometimes the person's body may slightly to aggressively vibrate until they are completely filled with His love leaving no place for darkness to return." Very Cool", usually changing the person's life by experiencing more healing, freedom and peace. If you belong to the Lord, don't believe any negative thoughts that He won't use you to set the captives free. Stop struggling with that LIE. The Lord is no respecter of people, although He may show favor to those who pursue His will. His desire is for us to be like Him and eventually grow to become One in Him. It's written, if you draw near to Me, I will draw near to you. The Lord gives us no excuses of His true word. We deceptively believe our own lie. Unfortunately, the believed lies holds us back eliminating ourselves as vessels from participating in the Lords life changing victories, as He sets the captives free.

CHAPTER 13

FISHERS OF MEN

In this chapter:
- Salvation and Setting the Captives Free
- Jesus Said, "Follow me, and I will make you become fishers of men."
- Filling Your (Salvation) Boat – Successful and Unsuccessful Ways to Fish

Salvation and Setting the Captives Free

Since 1992 and on through the years, even now, the Lord has given me divine appointments where He manifested His loving presence and touch 80% of the time – being faithful 100% of the time. Every second or third day consisted of an array of spiritual demonic activity. As I said earlier, I used to pray, fast, and petition, even beg the Lord for divine appointments to be involved in healing and deliverance. I wanted to learn how to pray effectively. I prayed for the Holy Spirit to sensitize my spirit to His Spirit so I could become highly aware (putting my spiritual antenna up) and recognize who my Heavenly Father wanted to reveal His heart to and possibly set them free.

It's easy for me to start a conversation with anyone about anything. It's equally as easy to direct a conversation so it includes part of my testimony or stories about my spiritual experiences. Once I begin telling others about my spiritual experiences they usually respond with one of their own life stories (good or bad) or they begin to talk about what I just spoke about. Then I nonchalantly say something like, "Did you ever feel the power of God or the Holy Spirit on you?" Usually they answer, "No." Then I say, "Do you want to?" If they don't respond quickly, I'll say, "It will only take a minute." Then I say, "I can pray and ask the Holy Spirit to come upon you in power and reveal Himself to you and your life will change because He is real." Usually they agree and allow me to pray for them.

Without further explanation, I have them repeat after me, a short prayer (See Salvation Prayer in the Appendix). I continue by putting my hand on their head and invite the presence of the Holy Spirit to come upon them in power. The Lord usually reveals Himself in a powerful way so that the person knows that they know the Lord's presence touched them. Sometimes they'll feel tingling, vibrations, or their eyelids will flicker. Or they'll feel radiating heat somewhere in their body usually where healing is needed. Sometimes darkness manifests in different degrees.

What the person doesn't realize is that they just accepted or rededicated their life to Jesus Christ as their Lord and Savior by repeating the simple Salvation Prayer. Now they are saved and any tormenting spirits like fear, anxiety, or sickness may leave. It may take a few days for them to recognize the difference in their life, but they will.

Jesus Said, "Follow me, and I will make you become fishers of men" (Mark 1:17).

When I fish, I cast out my line with a special lure - the Father's love. The fish, I mean the person attracted to the lure, may nibble or bite and eventually become hooked (meaning I have their attention) as I speak the Heavenly Father's heart to them. I lovingly but quickly reel them in intentionally getting them close to the boat. Then I reach over the side of the boat and gently put my gaff through their gills. The fish (the person) is now personally engaged and doesn't want to swim away.

Using my spiritual gaff, I slowly pull their head up and out of the dark waters asking the same questions as I just did, "Did you ever experience or feel the power of God come upon you? Would you like too?" Then without further explanation, I lead them into the same repeat-after-me prayer (See Salvation Prayer in the Appendix). Then I take the fish/person completely out of the dark water and put them in the boat. Now after becoming saved they have ears to hear the gospel and they are excited to understand and learn more about the Holy Spirit encounter they just experienced. It's very simple with the Holy Spirit orchestrating the whole thing. Just follow His leading.

Always let the Lord and His Holy Spirit lead your conversations. With His help and some practice it will be much easier to fill your boat. Keep in mind that if you're using the wrong lure and technique, you'll only catch a few fish or none at all.

Filling Your (Salvation) Boat –
Successful and Unsuccessful Ways to Fish

Many fishers of men (ministers) are unsuccessful because they waste too much time pre-qualifying the fish/person as ready-to-be-saved or not as they attempt to reel them in. They may even think they need to prepare the fish for salvation by giving them a short teaching thus, delaying the catch. They may also limit their catch by inviting them (the fish) to church first to hear more about repentance, forgiveness, and salvation before they get the fish saved and into the boat. Meanwhile the fish gets tired or distracted and eventually spits out the lure and swims away never getting close to the boat. The sad truth is that the opportunity to catch (save) that fish is lost. And when another fisher of men uses a similar type of procedure or method they typically won't bite. Some ministers use an unsuccessful approach over and over hoping and expecting different results.

Remember that the Lord is in control and He doesn't judge us or pre-qualify us. He receives us just as we are. He changes heart's and He is responsible for the results, not us (Titus 3:4-7).

One of my passions is to get every fish that bites or even nibbles into the boat. The Lord desires to lead every fish once they bite the hook to HIMSELF, by us reeling them in and getting them into the boat (or saved) as quickly as possible. After that, there will be plenty of time for the fish to receive Godly teaching and counsel.

Some ministers (fishers of men) get fish to bite their lure but as they begin to reel in the fish they preach a sermon which actually enables the fish to run out more and more line. Then slowly, these fishers of men begin to reel the fish in and again get distracted. Perhaps this time may involve other conversations with the fish (person or people) allowing them to run out the line even a little bit further from the boat. When the fisher of men believes that it's time to reel in the fish, he becomes excited only to discover that as the lure/hook gets reeled closer to the boat, the fish releases the lure and swims away. Unfortunately, sometimes we forget the purpose of our endeavor or the method we use is too time consuming. Sadly, the result is a salvation that wasn't offered and a fish that slipped away and less fish in the boat. If it takes too long to reel in the fish, they usually spit out the lure and go on their way. Another problem is that some ministers (fishers of men) of the gospel believe fish must be in the boat first before leading them to Christ. This means fewer fish and fewer salvations.

Personally, I don't like fishing. I don't have the patience to sit in a boat or fish from a dock because I can't see the fish near my lure in the dark waters. So, when it came time to learn how to become a fisher of men, I asked the Lord to show me how to catch fish fast. It's important to understand and catch this (no pun intended) in your heart.

Being fishers of men has everything to do with salvation and bringing others into the Kingdom of God. When we are saved, the light of Jesus Christ's presence in us shines in the spiritual darkness. His light crowds out or pushes the darkness to the side so that His Word of truth can enter. As we become more intimately in love with Him and healed from those issues that cover His love in our hearts, the brighter His light will emanate through us. We become vessels of His love and His light. Darkness cannot overcome that. It cannot extinguish the light.

Darkness is attracted to His light but doesn't understand why. It's because we have Jesus' presence, power and light radiating through us. We are His shining ones – Jesus' lures.

(Figuratively speaking) When I sit in my fishing boat, I realize that Christ in me is a bright light that attracts the fish (people) (Matthew 5:16, Psalm 18:28). They swim toward the light of Jesus in me so I can see them right next to the boat. I don't have to cast a lure out into the water because Christ in me is the lure and the unsaved and unsuspecting fish who are swimming in dark waters swim to Jesus Christ's bright light in me. Now they appear before Him in me. So, as I explained earlier, I lovingly reach down with my spiritual gaff in my hand and gently and kindly place it through their gills just bringing their head out of the dark water as I introduce myself.

"Hi, my name is Pat. What's your name? Have you ever felt the power of God on you?" Then I say, "Would you like to experience the Holy Spirit's power and presence on you?" Usually they answer, "Okay." Then without advertising their need to be saved, I quickly lead them in a short salvation prayer (See Appendix) and ask the Holy Spirit to come upon them in power. After that in Christ I spiritually pull them right out of the dark waters or out of the world of darkness. I pull them out quickly and unexpectedly from the grip of the enemy into the boat of salvation, the Kingdom of God's light. As I place the fish in the boat, I can easily talk with them about the Holy Spirit encounter they just experienced.

Sometimes a school of fish (a group) may be watching you from a short distance away. They recognize their friend's excitement after receiving the Lord as you put him into the boat. Suddenly to your surprise they swim over and jump into the boat too! They believed the testimony they heard and felt the presence of the Lord and they agreed with their friend's decision. I immediately have them repeat the short salvation prayer, asking the Lord to reveal Himself to them. I recommend they find a good Spirit-filled Bible-believing church to attend, so the Lord can continue His great work in their lives.

Another way to think about this is that you are the boat. So, it doesn't really matter where you catch fish. The fish could be your neighbors, family, friends, co-workers, and others. The Lord needs fishers of men. He needs laborers to bring in the harvest (His children). Jesus told his disciples, "The harvest truly is plentiful, but the laborers are few. Therefore, pray the Lord of the harvest to send out laborers into His harvest" (Matthew 9:37-38).

Pray every day and ask the Lord to give you divine appointments and favor. As a believer you can be a laborer in the field reaping a great harvest of souls and bringing them into a relationship with Jesus Christ. Through Him they can have life more abundantly here and eternal life in heaven (John 10:10). Our Heavenly Father wants all of His children to be able to come home to Him for eternity. The Lord has chosen and encourages us to take part and participate in His harvesting of souls. It's the miracle of eternal salvation that was fully paid for with the blood of Jesus Christ His Son. As they receive Him as their Lord they also receive His free gift of eternal salvation.

Allow yourself to be used as a vessel or instrument of the love of Jesus Christ. It makes your Heavenly Father's heart happy. Your rewards will be stored up in heaven waiting for your arrival. He desires all of His children to be saved. He wants to spend eternity with them in heaven.

The angels rejoice every time a person freely receives eternal salvation that Jesus paid for. They know that person is now a child of God and will be coming home to heaven when their life ends on earth. Spiritual victory is won, being one in Christ (Luke 15:10).

NOTES

CHAPTER 14

THE LADY ON THE FLOOR

In this chapter:
• Expand Your Faith in Supernatural Authority and Take More Prayer Risks

Expand Your Faith in Supernatural Authority and Take More Prayer Risks

I had just attended a one-day class primarily focused on teaching us how to minister and pray for others. There were about forty of us in the class and at the end of it we had the opportunity to practice what we learned and pray for each other. I prayed for a couple of people and when I finished, I noticed that many others were still involved in the prayer ministry. I walked to the back of the church and leaned my back against a column to watch and observe.

I noticed one lady was laying on the floor on her side constantly shaking as three people were on their knees praying for her. I watched them for about five minutes when a cool thought popped into my head. I wasn't sure if the Holy Spirit put the thought in my mind or if it was my own thought. The lady on the floor was about four car lengths away from me. As I watched her, I decided to whisper out and command the manifesting darkness (demon) to look at me. I had my doubts about the outcome, but my curiosity was stronger. I thought if nothing happens then no big deal because no one heard what I whispered out.

Again, it is very important to take a prayer risk when praying. It builds your confidence, especially when something happens. As you take a risk in praying for a supernatural response the Holy Spirit may show, teach, or reveal a secret of the Father's Heart in that area of your prayer request. It brings the word of God into your life's experiences. Philippians 4:13 says, "I can do all things through Christ who strengthens me."

As I was leaning against the column with my arms folded, looking at the lady on the floor, I whispered, "In the name of Jesus Christ of Nazareth, I command the darkness that is manifesting on the lady lying on the floor to look at me." To my disappointment, nothing happened. Well, it only made me more determined to try again. I could feel faith surging up within me as I whispered out again with more surety. "In the name of Jesus Christ of Nazareth, I command any demonic presence in or around the lady with the white hair lying on the floor to look at me now! And I rebuke any disobedience." Suddenly her entire body began shaking and trembling more intensely. The three people praying for her looked at each and began praying louder than before.

Remember, praying loudly doesn't threaten dark spirits (the enemy). It's the authority of Jesus Christ in you that they fear, especially releasing (in faith) the spiritual sound of the voice of Jesus through you as you speak. If you understand and catch the significance of His authority in your heart as being one in Christ, the darkness will tremble and usually manifest at some degree in your presence (Psalm 97:4). Sometimes it flees from the person as you walk towards them because the darkness feels exposed before you even say a word. Some leave as the bright light presence of Christ in you comes closer to them as long as the person didn't give the darkness permission/authority to stay.

I couldn't see the lady's face because she had her back towards me laying on her side on the floor. Once again, in a low forceful whisper, I repeated the same prayerful command adding, "I know who you are and your purpose (which I actually didn't) and I command you to look at me now in Jesus name!" She began to moan and shake more rapidly. "The enemy trembles at the mention of His (Jesus) name." I repeated it over again, "Now, look at me now!" All at once while intently shaking, she slowly turned her head and shoulders so that she could see me and looked directly at me.

I was still standing in the back of the room when her eyes appeared to be locked onto mine. Her eyes opened real wide as the manifesting dark spirit screamed in fear really loud with consistent, short bursts. As I started walking towards her, the people praying for her appeared unsure what to do. Midst the screams, two of the people praying for her stopped and stood up. I continued walking towards her with my eyes focused on hers as she continued to scream. As I got closer to her laying on the floor I could see that her face was a little contorted and full of fear (the manifesting demon). I knelt down next to her and I command it to be silent in Jesus name. Her screams became quieter, sounding like they were restricted, but her body continued to increasingly shake.

Her eyes were still flared open really wide and were fixed on mine. I gently covered her eyes with my hand so the darkness couldn't see me (Christ in me) as

I softly spoke to her. I broke the power of the dark spirit and commanded it to be still. Then I reassured her that everything was going to be OK. I immediately asked her while she was calming down, "What did you see and what did you hear?" Her voice was trembling as she answered, "Get away from you." She said, "I hear something saying, 'Get away from you.'" She began to cry and went on to say that she saw some black shadowy figures.

Some of the other prayer church class members were standing by watching and listening. The pastor asked us to bring her into the other room to continue ministering to her. We helped her up as we supported her and walked with her towards the nearby room. But the closer we got to the room, the more she began to manifest. She collapsed, losing all strength in her legs. It was as if the manifesting demon didn't want her to go into the other room. Darkness knows that when the Lord exposes them it won't be long before they are expelled and lose their secret acquired home. At that time I had her pray and rededicate her life to the Lord. After praying and breaking the power of the enemy's plan concerning her, we were eventually able to sit her on a chair in the other room.

While I asked a few questions, one of the women stood next to her with her arm around her shoulder to offer emotional support and some added stability to keep her from shaking herself off the chair.

Long story made short. The woman who was in her 50's admitted a lot of bad things happened to her. They started when she was around seven years old. Up until this point, she was unable to talk about what happened. She went on to tell us how she was sexually abused by a relative when she was seven years old and it continued a number of times throughout her childhood years. And then it continued with people she didn't even know until she was in her mid-twenties. She remembered feeling like she had an invisible sign on her that said, "Come rape me."

"I didn't understand what I was doing wrong and why people abused me," she explained. "I must have blocked out of my mind a lot of what happened." She told us that she had traumatic memory flashes of the "bad stuff" and it tormented her.

There were many secret issues she was hiding and unable to deal with. Without her knowing, the enemy took advantage of the secret traumas to construct a spiritual demonic stronghold upon her. There was unforgiveness and so much more. Many times, unspoken, hidden secret traumas we experience may give power to the darkness to torment us in various ways.

For the first time in her life as she spoke out what happened as the light of Jesus Christ exposed and consumed some of the darkness. The darkness was trembling and shaking while she was experiencing a portion of freedom (deliverance) and healing as she spoke out sins committed against her (into the light) for the first time.

Over the years starting as a child she developed coping mechanisms that hindered her development emotionally, mentally, and spiritually. She had numerous physical and mental handicaps. In an effort to protect herself she learned to intentionally become unattractive. She hoped that gaining a lot of weight, not wearing makeup or nice clothes, and staying home would keep her safe. In spite of her efforts, she was tormented with guilt, confusion, and self-hatred to the point of wanting to kill herself.

As a reminder, "The enemy comes to steal, kill, and destroy, but I (Jesus) have come to give life, and life more abundantly" (John 10:10).

It was amazing what the Lord did in one hour. All of us agreed that it was a good starting point for her and in the right direction. She told us that she was experiencing peace that she hadn't felt in a long time. Her face and countenance appeared more peaceful and the shaking stopped. We encouraged her to start attending a Spirit-filled, Bible-believing church and to continue receiving counseling and healing.

Time spent with a Christian counselor brings healing results that can be experienced much faster. True healing is usually obtained because the Lord heals the person's emotional and heart issues. It also saves years of secular counseling which is more about assessing and labeling a person with a condition. In secular counseling, adjusting and coping with the issues is often the priority versus true healing. And, unfortunately, prescription drugs are very prevalent and prescribed to take the edge off a tormenting issue which may result in unwanted side effects.

When a child experiences personal sexual abuse trauma in their early years, dark seducing spirits may attach themselves to the person or linger around them. The child doesn't realize that these sexual spirits attract other sexually perverted spirits to themselves. Since seductive sexual spirits are attached to other people for various reasons, this issue may cause unwanted sexual abuse encounters. Each child through life may be affected differently. Some shy away from sexual encounters in their adult lives while others have increased sexual cravings. Either way Jesus can heal and set them free from these dark spirits if they receive prayer.

This woman was likely tormented by a seductive sexual demon that attracted other sexual demonic spirits and cohorts that were attached to her abusers.

Experienced ministers can discern, pray, and release any attached seducing demons and attached soul ties with targeted prayer rebuking it in Jesus name. It's important to understand that the Heavenly Father loves all of His children and hates the enemy assaults along with Its stealing, deceptive work.

Nowadays sexuality is even more confusing than when I grew up. The enemy is having a heyday deceiving the younger and older generations. But on that day, the lady met the unconditional love of Jesus. He started to release her from the grip of darkness and deception and brought her into His presence and light. Two weeks later I heard that she joined a Spirit-filled Church that believed in prayer and healing through Jesus and the power of the Holy Spirit. She received Christian counseling for a year or so and is now a prayer person in her church. And she prays with understanding. She knows the hurts people carry who were sexually abused. The Lord continues to heal us as we minister to others. It's important to give away to another in need as the Lord's unconditional healing love has been given to us.

I have come to experience and recognize that through Christian counseling, Jesus can quickly heal people with life-long, deep issues if they want to be healed which is another story altogether. However, secular counseling (after a behavioral or mindset assessment) tends to label or diagnose a person with any number of disorders. And in this case, counseling would be primarily focused on teaching someone how to cope and manage their issues. The person is typically prescribed medications to help adjust behavior or thinking patterns to make their life more peaceful and manageable. Secular counseling also may focus on adjusting prescription dosages rather than on true healing.

Jesus heals people – inside and out. The only label anyone should receive concerning their lives is that they are a son or daughter of their Heavenly Father through Christ Jesus– the King of kings. All other labels are a distractive lie and can become a possible curse on your life and should not be received.

1 Peter 2:24 says, "He himself bore our sins" in His body on the cross, so that we might die to sins and live for righteousness "by His wounds you have been healed."

NOTES

CHAPTER 15

CHILDREN ABUSED BY THEIR FATHER OR FATHER FIGURE

In this chapter:
- Be Healed From Physical, Mental, or Emotional Abuse
- Experience How Much Your Heavenly Father Loves You

Be Healed From Physical, Mental, or Emotional Abuse

Adolescent children who've been physically or sexually abused by their fathers or father figures will often have difficulty relationally relating to their Heavenly Father.

As we minister to people for healing, we often start by asking, "How is your relationship with the Lord?" We also ask them if Jesus was standing here in the flesh, what would He say to or about them? And what would they say in response to Him or about Him? You'd be surprised what people say and how they secretly feel about God and themselves. Not realizing it, they deliberately short-circuit or completely shut off the connection between themselves and God in areas of their life. As a result, they are unable to give or receive the love of Father God in their life. This is "Ground Zero" and must be resolved first in a person's heart before any lasting healing process can begin. It's also possible that it can affect much more than that in a person's life.

I find that it's easy for those who believe in Jesus to have a personal relationship with Him. It's easy to say that they love the Lord! But some find it more challenging to say or confess that they are "In Love With The Lord." And yes, there is a difference between the two. As I have traveled around visiting churches to minister, I recognize the statement "I Love the Lord" has become a spoken church cliché to many. There is no heart-felt or true love desire connection relationship in their statement. Empty words. Obedience to His Word is more challenging in their lives because they are only mindful of Him on Sundays. The teaching of the

Heavenly Fathers Love for us is not ex-pounded much in many churches leaving a void in the hearts of the fatherless and beyond!

Broken heart hurtful experiences develops a heart that is cautious to love again. Some protect themselves by NOT allowing their heart to be vulnerable to love again because the fear of experiencing another broken heart or hurt in some way. Actually it can affect their heart from truly falling in love and experiencing the height and the depth that Jesus and the Father love has for them personally. Unaware to many, it's usually an unconscious decision that generally prevents them from accepting a future permanent relationship with someone else as fear secretly controls that part of their life.

Experience How Much Your Heavenly Father Loves You

Many people who were abused by their father or father figures, may have difficulty turning to Father God for help throughout adulthood. Thoughts buried deep in their heart may not trust or believe that their Heavenly Father has or will protect them as they question His love for them in particular areas of their lives. They have portions of emotional diversified transference of hurts, guilt, disappointments, anger, rejection, that they received from their earthly father's or father figure's abuse. They associate blame to their Heavenly Father for failing them in those areas. We must remember that the Lord gives everyone free will. He will not control people's behavior, but that does not mean He condones it. He speaks to us and convicts our hearts to change, but many follow their **own will** doing good or evil things. But they pray, trusting and wanting Jesus in their lives but shy away from their Heavenly Father, even knowing that Jesus, the Heavenly Father and Holy Spirit are ONE. "Jesus manifests the Father's love; the devil manifests the father's rejection". The enemy and its cohorts involved are sometimes deceitfully successful accusing Father God lack of love and concern in their thoughts during their abuse and afterwards, that some victimized people begin to believe. Truthfully, the blood of Jesus Christ was poured out for God the Father to redeem us. God is LOVE, and He cannot deny His own Word. Again, remember that Gods two Greatest Commandments are (1) Love the Lord your God with all your heart and with all your soul and with all your mind. (2) Love your neighbor as yourself (Matt 22:36-40). So, what do you think the enemy's focused goal is after, concerning the two "Greatest Commandments" scripture verses? The enemy's desire and tactics is to deceive them into believing the total opposite, lie and to reject God their Heavenly Father and deny Him their love. The enemy's intense deception may win over the abused person's angry unforgiving heart as their eyes are some-times unknowingly focused on the darkness in the enemy's camp. The enemy's strategy is to capture and keep the persons heart from forgiving, which gives darkness a continual secret spiritual open door to torment their heart and life in many possible ways. Unforgiveness is a sin opening a spiritual door for all kinds of spiritual and physical attacks, and it prevents the love of God from filling that area of a person's heart where healing is needed. Usually if the persons heart unknowingly continues to be focused towards the enemy's camp, the enemy may take an opportunity to steel, kill, and destroy a person's life without them recognizing it, being victimized again. Sometimes it takes years for the person to wake up and able to receive revelation of the deep passionate love that their Heavenly Father has been calling them to. Their back was turned to Him, and they had no ears to hear their Heavenly Father voice calling them to Himself. The enemy knew from the beginning that if the abused person captured the two Greatest Love Commandments in their hearts, that he (the enemy) would be toast in the persons' life. The person's heart and eyes would be focused on the Lord instead, bringing them healing, restoration to a long desired loving Father relationship with Him. This Father relationship becomes fulfilled in receiving their Heavenly Abba Father's Love, through Christ Jesus.

The Lord gave me a simple revelation on how to minister effectively to people trapped in this deception. You would think that people would understand the difference between their abusive earthly father and their Heavenly Father's unending true Love. But ministering to many, I realized that this is a hidden issue that needs to be addressed in the churches. Many abused by their fathers or father figures, have never received or experienced the Fathers love and actually crumble in tears as their hearts receive it. This also includes people who have attended church for years who live absent and totally unaware of receiving the deep passionate love that their Heavenly Father always has for them through Christ Jesus. His loving heart aches to spend time with His children. His true love fills those lacking or empty fatherhood areas in their hearts, bringing healthiness to them personally and as parents to their children.

When we all stand in heaven before our Heavenly Father, we will realize that He is the only TRULY GOOD, LOVING FATHER (Matthew 7:11). Everyone else is a sister and brother standing and worshiping Him in thankfulness. That means that your earthly father, grandfather, great grandfather are really your brothers in Christ (if they were saved). As you see them clearly through the eyes of truth (Jesus), you will recognize them as a brother (earthly fathers) who may have had many flaws. Many lacked the maturity of becoming a responsible loving father. Some examples may include; immature thinking as a parent, trapped in secret habitual sin, kept childhood negative angry attitudes, was also abused by their parents, thought negatively about themselves, had no idea or interest in being a parent themselves. Some fathers may have been continually absent from the family because of other reasons. They may have been employed by a company in a position that needed them to travel often, being absent weeks at a time. They may have had a government international position, keeping them away from their family for months, all causing a father relationship deficit to their children. Many adolescent's and adults feel resentment, anger and unforgiveness towards their father's absence during their childhood years. Their heart needs healing concerning this area, or their unhealed hurt may affect their own children in the future.

As children we look to fathers for support, stability, strength, guidance, love and kindness supporting a healthy family. There's no need to wait for heaven to recognize and receive the revelation that your Heavenly Father is a good Father and deeply loves you always, having His best intentions concerning you. He is "Love" and excitingly anticipates you being in Heaven with Him forever!! There is no comparison to an earthy father's absence, bad behavior or sin and evil deeds towards them, versus the overwhelming unending trustworthy true love of their Heavenly Father through Christ Jesus.

His truth becomes a choice to receive and live in this heart healing revelation OR chose to continue living apart and bankrupt of the Love your Heavenly Father has for you now and forever through Christ Jesus. The lying spirits of deception and Its cohorts will continue to secretly corrupt your thoughts and beliefs while eagerly smiling and laughing at your acceptance of its evil trap of lies.

CHAPTER 16

BLESSING THE WATER IN MY CUP = SPIRITUAL POWER

In this chapter:
- Taking Risks in Prayer, Accelerates Spiritual Growth
- Teach Me More Holy Spirit
- Break the Power of Negative Side Effects – Chemotherapy and Rx Medications

Approximately 150 people attended our Sunday services. Right after the services, people desiring prayer ministry would go to the front area of the church to receive prayer from the ministry team. Usually, eight to ten prayer team members committed to stay until everyone's prayer needs were met. It lasted anywhere from 2-3 hours.

One Sunday, I prayed for several people and eventually the prayer line dwindled down, there were less people waiting for prayer. A few of the other team members continued to pray. I went over to the water fountain and filled up a paper cup to drink. As I stood there drinking the water suddenly a woman who was being prayed for started to manifest and yelled out in anger. Apparently, she'd been manifesting for a while, but I was only aware of it when it became more intense. I slowly walked over there recognizing that four other ministry team members were standing with her praying and interceding. As I approached the woman from behind, I could hear the demon in a man's gravelly voice cursing and resisting the ministry. I stood a few feet behind her to listen to what was going on. I was still holding my now half full cup of water.

Taking Risks in Prayer, Accelerates Spiritual Growth

All of sudden I felt the Lord told me to use my fingers and flick some water from my cup onto her back. *Remember to be a risk taker even if you're not sure. The*

Lord will use these opportunities to reveal or teach you something. I dipped my two fingers in the water in my cup and without anyone noticing flicked the water from the tips of my two fingers towards her back. Nothing happened! The woman continued to manifest while the others continued praying for her. I figured there were enough people praying so I started to walk away. Suddenly a clear thought popped into my head, "Why don't you bless the water in Jesus name and try again?" I stopped and stood there thinking that the thought must be from the Lord and He was speaking to me. It wasn't my thought, and it came to me out of nowhere.

I blessed the water in the cup and dedicated it to Jesus Christ of Nazareth. I broke the power of any impurities and asked the Lord to purify it for use in deliverance. I walked over to the woman again and stood about five feet behind her. For the second time, I dipped my two fingers into the water and nonchalantly flicked it off the ends of my fingers releasing a few drops on her back.

WOW! This time she let out a roar like an angry animal! She lifted up her shoulder blades and arms as if I threw boiling water on her. She growled loudly and looked back over her shoulder at me. Her eyes were huge and bulging. The commotion caused everyone to stop and look in my direction. I shrugged my shoulders and played stupid and looked in the same direction (behind me) as the others were also looking to see what the manifesting demon was looking at.

No one saw what I did so they continued to minister to her. The enemy appeared to be playing hide and seek by manifesting and pretending to leave. I was only a member of this church for six months by this time. I attended every ministry training class that was offered.

I thought the woman's reaction was "cool" so I decided to try it again. This time from the front. There were still a few people praying with their arms and hands stretched out toward her. One of the ministers commanded the demon to go but it would respond in a creepy voice saying, "We own her! This is my house! You can't rebuke me!" This usually indicates the darkness has a legal hold or right to stay attached to an unconfessed sin like unforgiveness or something else.

In order to stand closer to her and not draw attention to myself I wiggled my way in between some others who were praying. I dipped three fingers in my cup instead of two, figuring it would be even more effective. I stretched out my arm and hand towards her in prayer like the others and eventually flicked the blessed water with my fingers toward her chest, and WOW! It happened again! The same demon popped out of its hiding place surprising everyone as it manifested again in its loud exaggerated, angry, animal-like sounds. The woman's eyes were super-wide and she showed her teeth and snarled at those standing near her. She looked at me and yelled again in a man's gravelly voice, "That burns!" (Again, I looked behind me as if she wasn't talking to me. No one knew why she was manifesting or what I did to cause the manifestation. I smiled to myself and thought, this is really cool!)

Teach Me More Holy Spirit

I walked away a few minutes later as people continued to pray and minister to her. About 45 minutes later I was getting ready to leave and the same woman walked up to me and asked what did I put on her? I said it was a few drops of water. She said, "No way!"

I told her I flicked some water on her with my fingers after I dunked them into my cup of water that I had blessed. She said it felt like burning acid shooting at her, and it felt like it burned clear through her body both times. She had a hard time believing it was only a few drops of water flicked off my fingers.

I asked her how she knew it was me? She told me whatever was inside of her knew. She said she felt pushed down inside and couldn't see most of the time. She had no control over what she (It) said or did. She could feel what the demon was feeling and knew it wanted to kill me, "…especially when you got in front of me and flicked the acid feeling water on it!" She could sense it hated my guts (big time) more than the others who were praying. I asked her if it left, and she said she wasn't sure, but she didn't think so. She wanted to speak to the pastor about it, because she never experienced uncontrollable darkness like that before. The pastor was outside talking with other members of the church as they were leaving. He wasn't there when she was receiving prayer.

About a week later I heard that she met with the pastor and received prayer and was set free from the darkness that attached itself to her. I learned she and her family were fairly new in the church. They had previously attended a church for years but they didn't minister to people in Holy Spirit power.

Break the Power of Negative Side Effects – Chemotherapy and Rx Medications

In the Gospel of (John 2:1-11) Jesus prayed and turned water into wine during a wedding celebration in the village of Cana. More people attended the ceremony than the wine caterers originally expected causing a wine shortage.

The Lord reminded me years later when I blessed my cup of water how it spiritually changed the water and the results when sprinkled on a person manifesting darkness. I was now diagnosed with symptoms of cancer resulting in administering four series of chemotherapy. I remember breaking the power of all unhealthy words or gestures that the doctors and staff spoke over me. I wouldn't receive any of it in Jesus name. I commanded the cancer and its cohorts to go back to the cross of Jesus where they were all defeated by Him in His death. Jesus said it is finished, and I stood and continue to stand on this belief.

I talked to the doctor prior to my first treatment. He brought in two different clear liquid chemo infusion bags and allowed me to pray over them, with my hands ten inches above, while they laid on a tray in his hand. Each time I prayed and blessed the chemo – breaking the power of any darkness attached to them and renounced all negative side effects. I dedicated all the chemo liquid content to Jesus Christ of Nazareth. I would only accept the good results from the doctor in Jesus name.

After each five-day biweekly series of infusions, I continued my tree service business using my aerial truck and equipment cutting trees down and trimming others. I had one more week series left when I felt a quick short electric shock go across the inside of my chest. I was in the aerial truck pushing a large log off the trunk of the tree. The next day I called my doctor to ask him about it. He said that he has no reference because people do not cut trees or do heavy labor when they are doing chemo. They just do chemo and nothing else. Although I did feel wiped out and tired at the end of each day which was not normal for me, I continued my business cutting trees each day for customer's.

I now pray over any medications and supplements that I may take, blessing them and breaking the power of any negative side effects in Jesus name. I also dedicate all the content in the medication and give Jesus Christ of Nazareth full authority over it. You have nothing to lose by praying over them and everything healthy to GAIN!

CHAPTER 17

THE MAN WHO ROLLED AWAY

(PART 1 OF 2)

In this chapter:
- Darkness Evades the Presence of the Holy Spirit
- Using Your Spiritual Authority in Christ

One of the more tedious aspects of owning and operating a tree service business is known as estimating. Tedious, but necessary. After working all day I'd get in my car with a list of names and addresses of people requesting estimates. Early evening and weekend appointments were preferred to ensure the homeowner was available.

As I mentioned in an earlier story, I'm always asking the Lord for divine appointments to minister to people. Looking at and estimating potential tree work jobs became one of the Lord's training grounds He used to teach me.

When I met with homeowners it always amazed me that within a short time they would begin telling me about their ailments, pains, injuries, and sicknesses. Sometimes the older folks would tell me about the high monthly cost of their medications and that they could hardly afford it living on social security. These conversations opened the door of opportunity to tell them part of my testimony and introduce them to my friend, Lord, Savior and Healer — Jesus Christ.

To reiterate: The Lord answers my prayers always giving me divine appointments. He will do the same for you almost every time. Actually, they are His divine appointments with His children. Jesus may be responding to their prayers by sending you! He can reveal Himself to them using you. Through Jesus we are His vessels and spiritual harvesters of souls. You have nothing to lose. Ask Him to use you and expect it to happen!

At this point I continue telling them more of my experiential testimonies that are related to their issues explaining to them what the Lord did for that person. I continue while looking at their tree job.

In this story I was estimating a potential tree job for a man named Joe. He showed me trees in his back yard to remove and wanted a price. I already had the cost of the job figured out in my mind as we continued talking and walking toward my car. As Joe and I walked to the front of his house his wife was standing on the side of the driveway talking with my wife, Rebecca, who got out of the car to meet her. As Joe and I approached them, I mentioned to Joe's wife that he was just telling me that he was recently diagnosed with cancer and has a follow-up appointment next week. She responded sadly, "Yeah, we are going to find out more information at the next appointment."

I summarized the conversation I had with Joe about Jesus Christ that He heals people as they come before Him in faith and expectation of His healing touch. Then I repeated some of my testimony stories to her. She really didn't say much in response. She just looked at her husband and shrugged her shoulders. Then I walked up to Joe and boldly said, "Are you ready?" He looked at me strangely and said, "Am I ready for what?" I said, "I'm going to pray for you and ask the Holy Spirit to come upon you and we'll see what He does." His face looked hesitant, so I told him that he had nothing to lose other than his cancer and everything to gain including a good doctor's report next week and a long healthy life!

I asked Joe to give me his hands and open them up to the Lord because He is standing right next to us. Matthew 18:20 says "For where two or three gathers in My name, there am I with them." Isaiah 41:10 says, "So do not fear, for I am with you; do not be dismayed, for I am your God. I will strengthen you and help you; I will uphold you with My righteous right hand."

I went on to explain that I am not the healer because it is written that I can do nothing of myself (John 5:30). Jesus Christ of Nazareth is the healer and is standing right here with us. Once again I asked him if he was ready. This time he nodded his head, "Yes."

I was initially going to have him repeat Parts 1 & 2 of the Salvation Prayer (See Appendix) but decided to ask the Holy Spirit to come upon him first. I put my hand gently on his head and said, "Come, Holy Spirit." He immediately seemed to be forcibly pushed backwards and fell pretty hard on the lawn. I quickly tried to grab his arm, to lessen his fall but it happened super-fast and I wasn't ready for that kind of response. He was probably in his mid to late sixties, so I was glad that he fell on the grass. The Lord protects us from injury anyways during times of ministry.

When someone falls backwards to the ground while receiving prayer it is referred to as being slain in the spirit. This happens because the strong presence of the Holy Spirit overwhelms them causing them to fall backward or forward depending on what the Lord is doing. There are many people who may not fall at all and receive just as powerful a touch and outcome as people who fall. Many people fall backwards intentionally as a minister touches them because they believe that is the correct response they observed from others. Some people's high emotional expectation may consume them and they fall before the Holy Spirit touches them. Either way, the Holy Spirit still moves powerfully.

Darkness Evades the Presence of the Holy Spirit

There is another reaction to prayer in the presence of the Holy Spirit that I refer to as a "false deception" of being slain in the spirit. Many church leaders/ministers are either unaware or deceived when the enemy uses this tactic. You can usually tell if the enemy may be at work when the person quickly falls or drops like a rock when you stand in front of them or when you place your hand on their head or after you ask the Holy Spirit to come and rest on them. Be aware of this unusually quick response and ask the Lord if the enemy is taking them out so that they won't be able to hear or receive the blessing or touch from the Lord. The spiritual gift of discernment operating in you will immediately clarify the issue if you are aware of the enemy's tactics.

When I experience this reaction in the past, I kneel down on the floor or the ground next to them and ask them if they can hear me. If they don't respond, I pray and break the power of a deaf spirit (as I mentioned in an earlier story). I ask them again, "Can you hear me?" If they say "Yes," then I know the enemy or darkness is trying to avoid being exposed or recognized evading the light of Jesus. I continue to question the person, "Do you feel or hear or see anything?" If nothing seems unusual, I continue to pray the same blessing upon them and see what happens.

If I discern that some sort of darkness is hiding or has attached itself to the person, I whisper and command it to leave or come into the light in Jesus name to see why it is there, or what is its purpose. I may work briefly with the person to get rid of it, bringing freedom to areas in their life. Sometimes in church, the prayer ministers may not have the necessary time to spend with someone who reacts to prayer in this way. Especially if there is a large number of people waiting for personal prayer. It's important to take note of who the person is so you can encourage them to get more prayer after the meeting.

Joe fell down like a rock after I asked the Holy Spirit to come upon him. When I knelt down on the ground next to him and reached out my hand to pray his body immediately stiffened and the enemy quickly rolled him away from me. It was as if the enemy didn't want me to touch him. He did three complete rolls causing his eyeglasses to sit sideways on his face. He had sprigs of grass in his hair and clothes.

I stood up, and again walked toward Joe to kneel down next to him. But as soon as I raised my hand he rolled away again stiff-backed with his face in the grass completing another three rolls away from me. It was almost comical! I was determined to pray for him knowing full well that the enemy was trying to keep him away from me (Jesus in me). At this point his eyes were closed and he didn't appear to be conscious of his evasive behavior.

His glasses were somehow still attached to one ear, hanging down across his face. I tried two more consecutive times without getting the chance to kneel down and pray before he rolled away. He rolled halfway across his lawn and eventually landed with his back up against the trunk of a tree. Since he was unable to roll any further when I knelt down to pray, the tormenting spirit of darkness caused Joe's back to arch around the trunk as far as it could go trying to get away from the presence of the Lord. His arms and legs were trembling and reaching back as far as possible away from me. It was unbelievable! If the tree wasn't there, who knows how far the enemy would have rolled him.

Using Your Spiritual Authority in Christ

The manifesting darkness was seeing Jesus Christ in me and it hadn't noticed that it backed Joe up against a tree. I took advantage of his inability to roll away and placed my hand on his heart. I prayed and commanded the darkness and all its cohorts to release him. I then broke the power of all its plans and games concerning Joe, his health, family and future. I also broke the power of any affliction, curse, disease or cancer in his body and proclaimed the blood of Jesus Christ over it including all dark spiritual roots. I commanded them to shrivel up and die in Jesus name.

Immediately Joe's body started to relax then it went limp. I declared that nothing of darkness could remain and commanded all spiritual residue to leave in the name of Jesus Christ of Nazareth. Then I asked the Holy Spirit to fill him with His presence and occupy every cell in his body. I also asked that Abba Father's perfect love would crowd out all darkness and fill every physical and spiritual void. As I continued to pray (as the Holy Spirit led me) the man seemed to wake up. Initially he was very confused and surprised about where he was — on his back and up against a tree in his backyard.

I told him to stay still for a few minutes because the Holy Spirit was still ministering to him. I encouraged him to relax by the tree for a little while. He told me that he felt a slight vibration throughout his entire body. I explained that this was the presence of the Holy Spirit upon him and that the Lord was healing and releasing him. I also took the opportunity to have him pray by repeating after me the Salvation Prayer 1 and 2 (See Appendix).

Someone taught me that if they are slain in the spirit, to stay and rest in the presence of the Lord until He is done ministering to them. Sometimes the Holy Spirit comes over people in a wave fashion effect washing over them bringing them deeper into His presence. You'll know when the Lord is done before you get up.

(continues in the next chapter)

NOTES

CHAPTER 18

DIVINE APPOINTMENTS CONTINUE

(PART 2 OF 2)

In this chapter:
• Joe's Wife Was Also Slain in the Spirit in the Backyard

Joe's Wife Was Also Slain in the Spirit in the Backyard

Meanwhile, I noticed Joe's wife, Sandra, looking shocked and confused standing at a distance with Rebecca. I quickly walked over and explained what just happened and that the Lord was releasing and healing her husband. He was tangibly touched by the Lord and was going to feel great. I told her that I encouraged her husband to stay in that place as the Lord ministered to him. I wanted her to know that the Lord was in control.

Then I asked her if she was ready, "Because the Lord wants to touch and reveal Himself to you, too." She looked at me and smiled as I reached down and took both of her hands. I didn't give her a chance to refuse. I asked her to look at me while I prayed asking the Holy Spirit to come upon her in power. I asked the Lord to release her from any heaviness that I sensed she was carrying possibly because of the concerns surrounding her husband's health.

As we prayed she suddenly started swaying slowly back and forth (slain in the spirit). She was becoming drunk in the spirit as she drank in the new wine of the Holy Spirit (Ephesians 5:18). Then down she went! I was able to hold on to her hands as I slowly laid her on the grass in the back yard. Rebecca and I knelt down beside her and blessed what the Lord was doing. She was so peaceful. It looked like she was unconscious, just lying in the grass.

I glanced over at her husband, Joe, who was still laying in the grass against a tree about 75 feet away in the backyard. I chuckled at the thought of their neighbors looking over and seeing them both laying in the grass with my wife and I (complete strangers) kneeling next to his wife. One person laying on the ground is alarming enough especially if they tripped or fell suddenly. But two neighbors on the ground looks like the result of something far more sinister. They could have thought that we mugged them or hurt them. Fortunately, none of the neighbors came running over and no police cars showed up.

Within about five minutes Joe's wife Sandra opened her eyes and sat up quickly. She appeared confused and didn't remember how she landed on the ground. We encourage her that everything was OK and that she was resting in the presence of the Holy Spirit. Thankfully, the couple attended a Spirit-filled Church and were familiar with being slain in the spirit. Later she told us that she had never experienced anything like this!

We helped her to her feet and she told us that she felt a little weak. This is common when the Lord and His Holy Spirit removes tormenting spirits or burdens that we are unknowingly carrying.

Matthew 11:28-30 "Come to me, all you who are weary and burdened, and I will give you rest. Take my yoke upon you and learn from me, for I am gentle and humble in heart, and you will find rest for your souls. For my yoke is easy and my burden is light."

It's not unusual for someone to feel extremely tired after being set free from spiritual aliments. As Sandra stood up, she looked over at Joe who also just got up off the ground. He slowly walked over towards us acting a bit confused. He did not remember any part of rolling away or even going down on the ground.

This is not unusual. Many people don't remember all the details of a Holy Spirit encounter regardless of how intense it is.

Sandra began to tell Joe what happened and he really didn't have much of a reaction to what she said. He was still a bit dazed by his Holy Spirit visitation. I explained to him that the presence of the Holy Spirit had a power encounter with some dark spiritual presence that was attached to him that didn't belong there. I told him that maybe the Lord released and healed him from his health issues among other things. I made a declaration, "We expect a good health report from next week's appointment with the Doctor," and told him to thank the Lord in advance for his complete healing. He agreed with everything I said.

He said he was still experiencing a warm sensation in his belly and chest area with a slight shaking or vibration. So I explained that was the presence of the Holy Spirit continuing the healing work inside of him and it could last for a couple of days. I told both of them that they will experience a greater peace now in many areas of their lives because the Lord is the Prince of Peace and His presence is resting on them.

I advised both of them to agree in prayer and faith every day, that Joe is healed of cancer and any other aliment. We talked for another ten minutes or so about what they just experienced and about their church background. Joe glanced down at his watch and was surprised by how late it was. They had a dinner date within the hour and cut our conversation short so they could get ready.

It's truly amazing to me how something as commonplace as dinner plans (in this case) can distract someone from continually experiencing a first-time, extravagant, life-changing, power-encounter with the Lord of Lords and King of Kings. It was as if nothing fantastic just happened. In many Holy Spirit encounters, a person will feel free immediately. They will feel released or healed and within a few days the effects will encompass and change many areas of their life.

To finish the story, although I knew the price for Joe and Sandra's tree job, we got so caught up in what the Lord was doing that I didn't give it to him. We didn't get a chance to discuss the price of doing the job. I stopped by the following week to see how they were and what happened at the doctor's appointment, but they weren't home. As I walked back to my car I prayed and came into agreement with their prayers for health and a good report from the doctors.

NOTES

CHAPTER 19

HOLY SPIRIT ENCOUNTER WITH MY EMPLOYEE, ALEX

(PART 1 OF 2)

In this chapter:
- Testimony and Observation Leads to Curiosity and Salvation – Resulting in Healing and a Changed Life
- Being Mentored Accelerates Spiritual Growth

Owning and operating a tree service for more than 40 years was a challenging and fulfilling job that brought a host of interesting characters into my life and business. Because of the flexibility and physically demanding nature of the work my crews were a mix of muscle heads, renegades, rebels and ex-cons. They were all hard workers like myself and I was proud to watch them professionally perform their work duties as customers and neighbors watched.

As you already know I love telling teachable Holy Spirit stories. Not made-up ones, but the ones about how the Lord transformed my life by turning my world right-side-up which felt up-side-down to me (Isaiah 29:16) for at least nine months after I truly received Jesus into my life…but that's another story.

I took advantage of every opportunity to tell my customers and workers stories about the Lord and how the Holy Spirit touched and revealed Himself to me and others I prayed for. Some of the guys on the crew witnessed me praying for many customers and observed first-hand the manifesting power of the Holy Spirit.

Testimony and Observation Leads to Curiosity and Salvation – Resulting in Healing and a Changed Life

One day we finished a job early, around noon. Alex, a new employee and friend, wanted to talk to me about something. He worked with me for about three weeks and told me that he'd been listening to my testimony stories. At first he didn't believe they were true. Only after seeing my genuine excitement every time I told, what he considered, "another unbelievable story," was he convinced that I was telling the truth. I told him that sometimes I have a problem believing everything that happens as the Holy Spirit moves on people!

We were standing by his car after work and Alex kept talking to me about his concerns. He said a couple of the stories I told him last week reminded him of his mother. "Sometimes if she gets drunk she'll talk to an invisible person as if they are standing right next to her," he said. "If she tries to walk and falls down, she'll yell out, 'Who pushed me down?'" Or she might say, "Stop pushing me on the floor!" Alex wanted to know why this was happening. He wondered if this could be a dark spirit.

I told him that there could be any number of natural and spiritual issues at work in the situation. Unfortunately, he didn't think his mom would want to talk to me or let me pray for her. When we finished talking about his mom, Alex asked me to pray for him, if I had the time.

He explained that for many years he had experienced on occasion an irrational fear. When he listened to my stories he felt the same fear rise up so intensely that he wanted to walk away in the middle of my story. He felt embarrassed knowing that something was going on inside of him. Trying to make sense of things he wondered if the fear somehow came from his mother. I told him that I didn't know, but we could pray and ask the Lord and see what happens. He said, "OK," but he insisted that we move near the shed behind the house so the other workers wouldn't see him as they were heading home after working. We were at my parent's house property where all of my equipment and tree trucks are parked.

He asked me, "How do you know all this stuff?" I told Alex, I have been going to a Spirit-filled, Bible believing church that greatly valued teaching and releasing people to be used in Holy Spirit power evangelism. I also attended many ministry classes in the church that taught me about knowing your spiritual authority, who you are in Christ and how to pray/minister to people. I regularly asked the Holy Spirit to teach me how to pray effectively so that the Lord would manifest and reveal Himself to people He places in front of me.

Being Mentored Accelerates Spiritual Growth

My pastor was a humble, charismatic Holy Spirit powerhouse, a true shepherd of shepherds. If I were to describe him in a few words, it would actually be very simple. There are many parts of the Body of Christ, but one part is not greater than the others. His part was the Father's Heart "Love", which gives desire and power to move all the other parts of the body in ministry. He operated out of the heart of God. He was one of my mentors. He told me that learning about God's love for you is one thing, but to accelerate your spiritual growth and be more effective in ministry, he said, "You have to catch the word of God and the Father's Love for you (and others) in your heart." It's essential that you fall deeply and intimately in love with your Heavenly Father through Christ Jesus. It's essential that you receive His love, that you own it and become it, then releasing it as a vessel of the Father's love that can be poured out to those in need. POWERFUL!!

I had another exceptional mentor and his wife (Lew and Shari Ackerman) who helped initiate my Holy Spirit, encounter-filled journey. They exposed me to their Holy Spirit stories concerning witchcraft, multiple personalities, and other types of power encounters. Both informed me about the depth of spiritual ministry that I never heard of before. They invited me to their weekly evening prayer meeting at their house. I witnessed and learned from their ministry by observing deliverance manifestations and counsel that captured my interest and attention. They are positioned on the front lines in the Army of God. They invited me to their Spirit-filled church where they both were christian counselors. After meeting their pastor and attending a Holy Spirit retreat, the Lord planted me there to learn more. The pastor and my two counselor friends were a POWERHOUSE of spiritual authority and understanding, easily setting the captives free. I can write another book just on what I learned and experienced from their mentorship. UNBELIEVABLE!

The fastest way to truly fall in love with the Lord is to spend time in His presence in the "secret place" and to fast and pray. Ask for His Hunger and Thirst continually. Seek and desire to fall in love with Him naturally and spiritually. He will draw you all the more. He'll captivate your heart to Himself and consume you with His everlasting love. It's written in James 4:8 that if you draw near to God, He will draw near to you! But in His nearness to you, seek a deeper place in Him that leads to ONENESS of His Heart. Then start to live out of that life changing place.

The Holy Spirit powerfully reveals the demonstrated love of the Heavenly Father's Heart for His children through Jesus, through you, to those in need. The Holy Spirit is part of the Godhead or Trinity and is one in the Father and Son (John17:20-23).

Alex asked me, "How do you know when someone needs prayer?" Usually someone just asks for prayer. Sometimes I'll hear them talking about issues or problems they are dealing with and realize they need prayer for healing, physical or mental. Sometimes I see a manifestation of darkness, so I may approach someone and engage in a conversation and go from there as the Lord leads.

When I first started looking for people to pray for I missed a bunch of opportunities. My church was a safe place to practice prayer ministry and it was highly encouraged. The Lord would draw my attention to those who needed prayer. I would sometimes send someone else to pray for them with a few instructions from the Lord instead of going over to them myself. One time I told a person to go over and put their hand on a lady's stomach (with her permission) and wait, because within 30 seconds she'll burst out crying. And that's exactly what happened.

Another time I asked someone to walk over to a man standing next to the wall and say, "The Lord wants to heal and bless your childhood." Then wait ten seconds and place your hand on his heart (with his permission) and say, "Lord Jesus, heal his broken childhood heart." I guaranteed that his emotions will erupt and he'd cry really hard as the Lord released the hurt and pain he'd carried for a long time. Again, that is exactly what happened.

When the Lord shows you something beforehand this is a gift of the discernment or a word of knowledge (Proverbs 2:6).

Alex and I kept talking. I told him about two intercessors who came to me one Sunday and told me that the Lord wanted me to pray for Godly boldness. They told me the Lord has things for me to do, but I will need to pray and operate out of Godly boldness. I never heard of "Godly boldness" before. So I fasted and prayed for the Lord to give me His Godly boldness so I could speak His truth to people without fear.

Approximately two weeks later in church I discerned that a visitor was dealing with some issues, so I went over and talked to him about it. It didn't seem like a big deal to me until two members of my church, one who was a friend of the visitor, came over to me smiling. They said, "Wow, we can't believe what you said to him. Man, you're bold! You were even pointing your finger at his chest while you were talking to him." They told me that when I walked away the man told them he heard the Lord's voice speaking to him. He knew it was the Lord because there was no way that I would have known anything about him.

I left the church that day with a slight smile on my face realizing that the Lord was answering my prayer. I thanked the Lord for giving me Godly boldness to speak His heart to someone as He revealed the issues He wanted to release him from. He wanted to heal this man (1Corinthians 12:10).

As I stood longer with Alex near the shed in my parents' backyard, I told him that I was going to pray for him and see what the Lord wanted to do. Alex wanted to experience the power and presence of the Holy Spirit that he heard me speak about all the time. I placed my hand on his forehead and asked the Holy Spirit to come upon him in power and reveal Himself to Alex.

In a couple of minutes Alex's body started trembling. He stood with his arms held out in front with his hands open to the Lord and his eyes closed. I prayed and broke the power of the spirit of fear that would try to rob Alex from experiencing the power and presence of the Holy Spirit.

After I prayed I left him alone with the Lord with his body trembling more intensely. I went inside my parents' house and made myself a sandwich for lunch. About 15 or 20 minutes later I went back outside and Alex was still standing by the shed trembling (Psalm 99:1-5). As I walked closer to him I noticed tears streaming down his face. I quietly whispered in his ear, "Just stay where you are. The Holy Spirit is upon you and healing you from issues from your past. Continue to give the Holy Spirit permission to go deeper into your heart." I prayed and came into agreement with everything that the Holy Spirit was doing. In a whisper I told Alex again to stay before the Lord until He was finished and that he would know when He was done. I left Alex alone with the Lord again.

When I walked back into the house, I noticed my mother looking intently out the back window. She was staring at Alex who was still standing near the shed with his arms held out perpendicular from his body with his hands open. She was too far away to see that he was shaking intensely, and tears were streaming down his face.

My mom was raised in the Catholic Church and taught Sunday Catechism years ago. I could see that she was confused with a puzzled look on her face. To help her understand I explained that Alex was OK and that the Holy Spirit was healing him. I knew she would understand then, because it was almost every day that I'd be telling my parents about the many crazy God-stories and things that happened when I prayed for people.

(continues in the next chapter)

NOTES

CHAPTER 20

SEEING ALEX'S GODLY VISITATION IS BELIEVING

(PART 2 OF 2)

In this chapter:
- Jesus Draws People to Himself
- The Lord Says, You Will Be My Witness and Testimony Throughout Your Life

I came to an understanding when people physically see the Holy Spirit or darkness manifest on someone or themselves, it makes a quick believer out of them. As I was explaining and telling my mother about some other experiences I had with the Holy Spirit I realized that another thirty minutes had passed. I quickly stood up and looked out the window to check on Alex and smiled as I saw him still standing in the exact same position. I had to laugh at my mother's concern. She thought he fell asleep standing up or maybe even died. I asked her to come outside with me and walk over to Alex so that she could see the power encounter (trembling) that he was experiencing. We stood about 15 feet away and observed him for a few minutes. His body was still trembling but not as intense as before.

Jesus Draws People to Himself

Suddenly he wiped his face with his right hand and looked around for about a minute in the opposite direction. He stretched a little and turned in our direction. He saw my mother and I standing nearby and said, "Man, Pat, that was cool!" He told us that he felt his body shaking but couldn't move. At one point he felt heat that gradually intensified and made him sweat. I asked him if he heard or saw anything? He said he heard what I said to him but nothing else. I should have asked him what did I say? I learned that sometimes the Lord speaks to the person (through my voice) and they hear something totally different than what I said.

Alex said the sunlight was bothering him because it was shining in his closed eyes. When I told him the sun wasn't out or shining today, he was blown away. Usually the bright light they may see with their eyes shut is the Holy Spirit or Jesus standing in front of them.

I've seen this bright light several times when I was praying. On two of the occasions it happened in my bedroom in total darkness while I was laying on my bed praying. My eyes were closed and suddenly in the top left of my peripheral vision appeared an orange/gold light in the distance. It became brighter and brighter as it descended from the high left and instantly became a very bright white light that rested in front of me intensely on my face.

I quickly opened my eyes and saw nothing but the dark room. I knew it was a spiritual encounter with the Lord, but a doubtful thought motivated me to get up and look out the bedroom window to see if a car headlight or powerful flashlight shined in my window. Of course, no one was there. The position and angle of the window would have made it impossible for light to shine on my face anyway.

I laid down again seeking the light of the Lord's face and within five minutes the same thing happened. This time the light became so intensely bright that even with my eyes closed I squished them even tighter. It didn't lessen the intensity of the white bright light. I felt a slight heat on my face. My eyes felt like they were flickering as I turned my head to the side to tolerate the brightness. I thought to myself, "This is unbelievable!" Once again, I quickly opened my eyes to see only a dark room. For a second time, I jumped up and looked out the window and saw nothing.

I went back to lay on my bed and thought about the experiences I was having. I believed it was the Lord and decided to prepare myself with a different attitude. I asked Him to forgive me for allowing doubt to flood my mind concerning His presence. I told Him I desired to see Him face-to-face through His bright glory light and I invited Him to come back and visit me. I prayed for ten more minutes and then the same thing occurred. His light was super bright and white. I struggled to not turn my head away this time as I spoke to Him. My eyes were tightly closed and flickering in reaction to the light. I could feel the slight heat on my face and vibration in my body as the brightness caused tears to roll down both of my cheeks filling my ears. I felt such a deep peace over me. I accidentally opened my eyes and saw nothing but my dark bedroom. My body continued to experience His presence as my body vibrated slightly most of the night. The brightness of His light did not return that night.

This type of visitation occurred four other times while I was praying and seeking His presence. Twice it happened in my old bedroom at night in my parents' house. The other times were during the day while praying, but it wasn't as blinding bright. It's important to mention that everyone should be aware that Satan can also appear as an angel of light, but he is not full of peace or truth (2 Corinthians 11: 13-15).

I asked Alex how long he thought he was standing there. He said, "About 10 minutes." I smiled and told him it was a little longer than that. He guessed again saying, "No more than fifteen minutes." At this point, his body was still vibrating or trembling slightly. I explained that this is the Holy Spirit continuing to work in him and that it could continue into the next morning or even for a couple of days as he continues to seek the Lord.

Then I told him he was standing in the same spot for about an hour or more. He refused to believe that was true until my mother spoke up and confirmed the time. I know it's hard to believe because the same thing happened to me years earlier as I received prayer at a men's retreat. The only difference was that I fell backwards and was laying on my back on the floor. I had a few more strange experiences than Alex had at the time. I'll write about those later. Like Alex I also believed that I was only on the floor for 10-15 minutes when it was actually 1 ½ hours. My pastor explained to me that I had a spiritual experience or visitation with the Lord and that time doesn't exist in the spirit realm as we know it.

The Lord Says, You Will Be My Witness and Testimony Throughout Your Life

Alex was all smiles as he told us about his spiritual encounter with the Lord. He felt lighter and happier. I told him he felt lighter because the Lord set him free from all kinds of stuff that he was carrying around for years. We listened to Alex for about ten minutes and he said, "You know, even though I feel great, I'm starting to feel tired and wiped out." This is very common. In his case the intense trembling was the presence of the Lord confronting the darkness that was attached to him resulting in a power encounter (Matthew 21:12). The heat that he felt was the consuming fire of the Lord burning away everything that didn't belong in him or upon him (Hebrews 12:29).

Many times a person's body trembles or shakes during the initial deliverance. Then you pray again and ask the Holy Spirit to fill every void or empty place where the enemy once occupied. Sometimes the person shakes erratically or even violently as the Holy Spirit fills all those empty spiritual voids with the presence of God and His perfect love. The rapid infilling of His love overwhelms them. Usually we see this trembling or shaking when the Lord's love fills a large vacant area in the person where an occultic or demonic stronghold previously attached itself. An undiscerning minister may believe it's another demonic manifestation and try to cast it out or even stop it.

Sometimes due to the rapid infilling of the Holy Spirit and Father's love, the person not only feels extremely lighter but may have a floating sensation making it hard to walk normally for a little while. They slowly lift one foot at a time. The upward momentum of raising their foot may give them the feeling that it will continue to float upwards as they struggle to place it back on the ground. I observed this reaction in prayer ministry a few times.

One time was when a woman was released from an angry, murderous spirit. She most likely received it when she and her husband were involved in deep occultic practices fifteen years earlier. After the Lord set her free, she struggled to open her eyes because the natural light was too bright for her. It was afternoon and the ceiling lights in the room were not on because the windows let in enough light. We borrowed a pair of dark sunglasses from a church member so that she could open her eyes. She had been living in a dark spiritual cloud without even knowing it. Once the Lord set's you free, you are free indeed (John 8:36).

As she attempted to walk out of the room, she quickly grabbed the person standing near her. She felt like she was going to float up and away. She asked the person that she grabbed along with someone else to walk on either side of her holding her arms so she wouldn't float upwards. She took short deliberate steps slowly raising each foot about two feet off the ground. It looked like she was trying to walk through a two-foot-deep snow drift in slow motion. If those two people weren't holding her up, she would have likely lost her balance and fallen backwards onto the floor.

Eventually, someone brought her a chair to sit on because she had only taken ten steps in five minutes. Even when she was sitting on the chair she still felt as if she was going to float away. She asked one of the people helping her to stand behind her with their hands on her shoulders to hold her down on the chair. Within thirty minutes I saw her walking around normally but still wearing the dark sunglasses.

Now, getting back to my friend Alex. After I explained and answered some of his questions concerning his encounter with the Lord, I told him that this experience not only changed him but also changed some of his beliefs. When your beliefs change so does you're thinking and attitudes. Other people will notice.

I told Alex to ask the Holy Spirit to come and manifest Himself in and upon him again when he went to bed that night. He needed to forgive everyone who ever hurt or offended him and also forgive himself before the Lord. I encouraged him to start an intimate heart relationship with the Lord to draw closer to Him in a tangible way. As James 4:8 puts it, "Draw near to God and He will draw near to you."

Alex called me the next night and was super excited to tell me that he slept like a baby and felt really good. He called everyone he could think of and told them about his experience with the Holy Spirit. After hearing his story some of his friends and even his mother wanted prayer. Alex had more questions and told me that he hoped he would be confident to pray for people, too. I explained that the Holy Spirit is the same in everyone and wants to lead them into all truth which sets them free (John 16:13). Over the next few weeks he arranged for me to meet and pray for his friends and coworkers from his other job during their break time.

It becomes very time consuming because there is a huge need in the world today. People want to be healed and set free from many issues and they want to truly know and experience the Lord's love for them. A life can change right in front of you for the better as the Lord reveals Himself to them. It's priceless. Their desire to receive Him or rededicate their life becomes a non-issue.

NOTES

CHAPTER 21

A SALVATION PRAYER, A SPIRITUAL BATTLE, A BRIGHT FLASH, A LOUD EXPLOSION AND A GREAT VICTORY

In this chapter:
- Gods Calling Confirmed and My Decision to Accept

Gods Calling Confirmed and My Decision to Accept

I owned a piece of property at one time that had two small houses situated on approximately eight acres. I lived in one and advertised the other house for rent. One early evening a couple scheduled an appointment to look at the house. They arrived an hour later and I showed them the house. After viewing the house and property they came back to my house to give me a small deposit, a rent down payment to hold the house for them. They made arrangements with me to pay the remaining balance in two days.

They gave me a clear impression that they were married. I have learned not to rent to unmarried couples because they break up easily and when one of them leaves, the other is unable to pay the total monthly rent. As they were both standing in my kitchen I started talking about the Lord and how quickly He can reveal Himself and change lives. I spoke to them about a four-line short prayer that they could repeat after me asking Jesus into their heart as their Lord and Savior. I told them I would pray a short blessing over them after that if they wanted me to. The husband said, "Sure." He didn't have a problem with that. But his wife was a little skittish and seemed reluctant. So, the husband received the Lord by repeating a short prayer of salvation. Then the husband gave me permission to pray a short blessing over him and allowed me to put my hand on his head as I prayed. They both slightly bowed their heads and closed their eyes as I started to pray. I asked the Holy Spirit to come, and suddenly I felt a short burst of air flow under and over my hand, flowing through his hair causing it to blow in an upward direction (John 3:8). He immediately opened his eyes and looked at me strangely as if I blew on his forehead and hair. By the expression on his face I knew what he was thinking. I responded and said, "I didn't blow on you. That was the Holy Spirit." His wife immediately opened her eyes after she heard me speak to her husband. I just shrugged my shoulders and said, "You must be a blessed man." Then I continued to pray with my hand back on top of his head as if it wasn't a big deal. He closed his eyes again, but his wife kept her eyes open and seemed to be intently watching and listening to me.

As I continued to pray a blessing over him I thought to myself, "That was cool, Lord. I never experienced that before." I asked the Holy Spirit to breathe or blow His wind on him again (John 20:22)! I stepped further to the left of him and turned my head away from him as I prayed. This way if it happened again he would definitely know that it wasn't me blowing on him. Suddenly, it happened again! As I had my fingertips on his head, a short burst of air blew under and over my hand again pushing his hair up for a second or two. His eyes quickly opened and looked at me noticing my head was to the left of him and facing away. I said, "Did you feel that? It was either the breath of God or the wind of the Holy Spirit." I heard the slight blast of air and felt it under my hand. It sounded like a low strong short puff of air that you would hear come out of someone's mouth with some force behind it. It reminded me of another time that I had the same experience as a puff of air blew into my left ear twice one night as my pastor was releasing a powerful impartation of the Holy Spirit. It consisted of the healing and deliverance that he carried and operated in for years. My pastor believed the Holy Spirit blew in my ear to open it, so that I could hear the Lord's voice clearly.

His wife said she saw his hair blow back and confirmed to him that it wasn't me. Well, that second manifestation ended the prayer. I said, "I believe the Lord has His hand on you, so expect the Lord to reveal Himself more and more in your life." He smiled at me and agreed what just happened was pretty cool. But his wife seemed to receive a touch of fear and appeared anxious to leave. In a few minutes they were walking out of my house heading to a diner.

Sometimes the Lord moves powerfully upon people. Obviously, the Lord loves to reveal His manifesting presence that spiritually awakens us to His existence in our lives. He absolutely hates darkness and its destructive work upon His children. No darkness manifested with this couple nor did I discern anything. The Lord usually unexpectedly exposes any darkness causing it to manifest in some way. His bright presence in us as we speak in His authority quickly expels darkness in people. Sometimes as people I minister to see this, or experience it, they'll ask, "Who are you anyway?" I can discern their thoughts and respond letting them know, "I can't do anything of myself (John 5:30). The Lord Jesus Christ and the Holy Spirit's bright light presence and authority reveals and removes the darkness setting people free. He exposes and destroys the evil games and plans the enemy has against His children." Demons or darkness will speak to the thoughts of people you are ministering to. They will try to convince them that you are the evil one and try to sway them away from you.

But the Lord makes the enemy or darkness toast in His presence. I have so many true and intense experiences concerning the enemy's invasive attacks. I'll write about them in a sequel to this book to expose more tactics of the enemy and how the Lord led me to minister to those issues. The Church is the Army of the Lord and teaching stories and books are essential for those who battle on the front lines in the Lord. Those who read them will have more insight, confidence and knowledge of the enemy's strategies and works. The Lord in you does the battle for you! It's true. What took me years to learn and experience I'm trying to expose to facilitate one's walk as an effective warrior in the Army of God.

Back to the story...

An hour after the couple left my house, I received a phone call from the husband. He very politely asked me if he could talk to me concerning something strange that just happened to him. He said, "I didn't know anybody else to ask or who would even believe me. Since you just prayed for me, well, I think it has something to do with it." I asked him to tell me what happened.

He said they went straight to the diner after leaving my house. They were seated in a booth and he went inside the bathroom to wash his hands. He was standing in front of the big mirror when he saw a blinding bright flash of light with a very powerful loud sound of an explosion as his body shook. He thought someone detonated a large bomb in the restaurant. He said he believed his girlfriend (revealing to me that they weren't married) and all the people were blown up and dead. He rushed out of the bathroom door to help his girlfriend if she were still alive. To his surprise everybody was sitting, eating, and talking with no disturbance at all. His girlfriend was sitting in the booth where he left her. He said it was very strange and he had never experienced anything like this before.

I told him not to be afraid "Something very good just happened concerning you. Two hours ago you received Jesus Christ into your life to be your Lord and Savior. Prior to that you obviously belonged to the enemy, the father of lies. As you were in the bathroom standing in front of the mirror there was a battle in the spirit in the heavens over you and concerning you. The Lord allowed you to experience and see a part of it. Darkness did not want to let you go! But since you received Jesus Christ as your Lord, you now belonged to Him. The Lord's jealous love for you was enacted. His angelic army fought for you and defeated the rebellious enemy on your behalf. The bright flash explosion was a clash in the spirit between light and darkness and the angels of God destroying the enemy." He said, "That's very cool."

I told him, "The Lord has plans for you as you continue to surrender your life to Him." John 10:28 says, "And I give them eternal life, and they shall never perish; neither shall anyone snatch them out of My hand."

"The Lord will start revealing Himself to your heart. And there will be so much more," I added. "Make sure your girlfriend receives the Lord, otherwise, in a short time you will grow apart (2 Corinthians 6:14). As you abide in the Lord, He will teach you and you will become a man after His heart." I told him that everything I was speaking to him will happen. The timing depends on his obedience as he hears and obeys the Lord.

I told him to call or visit me anytime when he moves into the house rental and I would be glad to help him. I knew he was a little overwhelmed, but he had a great experience that night for confirmation. Yet I knew he could choose his girlfriend's path of fear and concerns and decide to follow her advice in a different direction. I knew that decision wouldn't last in the long haul because the Holy Spirit would continue to speak to his heart.

They never moved into my rental house. I never saw them again. He called a few days later and apologized that he was not able to rent the house from me. He told me to keep the small rental deposit of four hundred dollars. I encouraged him to come and get his deposit. It would be here for him. But I never heard from them again. When I think about them I pray a "hedge of protection" (Job 1:10) over them and ask the Lord to continue to reveal Himself to both of them.

CHAPTER 22

RICKY'S LIFE-CHANGING STORY
(PART 1 OF 4)

In this chapter:
- Accelerated Transformation Through Holy Spirit Power
- Simple Faith Grows A Powerful Godly Warrior
- Spiritual Life Goes From Rags to Riches – In Power

Accelerated Transformation Through Holy Spirit Power

Ricky worked for me on and off for many years cutting trees. He was raised in a broken home where alcohol was more prevalent than money and support. At a young age he was placed in reform school, but he ran away after a few months because of the rules and regulations. He continued to make many bad decisions through the years. Life now in his 40s was hard. He was always in and out of prison.

Ricky was a big guy with blue ink (prison tattoos) on most of his body. He told me many stories about his life "on the inside" as he called it. He stated that on a number of occasions in prison he spent time in the hole or solitary confinement for fighting among other things. He said the guards wouldn't give him any toilet paper in the hole, so he would tear out pages from the Bible that was in there until there weren't any pages left.

He described how his angry attitude continually made him use curse words against one of the correction officers who retaliated by spitting in his food before he pushed it into his cell hole. As Ricky told me his stories he would instantly be talking in an angry rage. He said, "I used to kick the food tray against the wall!"

Ricky was on parole when he worked for me. On a number of occasions, he was jailed for parole violations, but he'd be released soon after because of a lack of evidence or the parole officer in charge of him showed mercy. Otherwise, he would have had to go back to prison to finish his previous sentence which could be a couple of years.

Ricky was a good worker cutting trees and always on time. Many times I laughed to myself when he got poked in the leg by a dead stubby branch still attached to a down tree. Instant raging anger emerged and he would kick aggressively at the dead branch trying to break it off sometimes injuring himself.

I'd yell over to him, "Relax. Stop acting like a crazy man and cut it off with the chainsaw!" Then he'd walk over and pick up the chainsaw and pull the starting cord to start the saw. Usually it starts on the second pull, but this time Ricky had to continue pulling the cord to start the saw. His anger started to excel with every unsuccessful cord pull. Eventually on the 7th or 8th tug the chainsaw started. In his anger Ricky intentionally squeezed the trigger tightly and the chainsaw revved wide open as he walked toward the dead short tree branch gritting his teeth. He slammed the revving chain saw blade on the 2-inch diameter branch cutting it off in an instant. His anger continued raging as he cut off the four-foot branch that poked his leg, then three more consecutive times as it laid on the ground. I yelled while walking over to him saying, "You have to calm down and relax or you can't work with us anymore." I told him he was a danger to himself and to the other workers around him.

The Lord sends me divine appointments to teach me patience and provide direction so He can reveal Himself to someone in need "including me". He uses me as His vessel as He changes a person's life. Ricky's story is one of many great life-changing true stories where the Lord used me.

Without Ricky realizing it, I had spoken many life-related Scriptures to him and over him nonchalantly in our conversations. I'd respond to his questions saying, "It is written…" and follow that by speaking the fitting or circumstantial Scripture I'd memorized throughout my walk with the Lord. Then I'd release the Scripture words I had spoken over Ricky to the Lord knowing the Lord would fulfill that Scripture in His timing upon Ricky's life.

Isaiah 55:11 – So shall my word that goes out from my mouth: It will not return to me empty but will accomplish what I desire and achieve the purpose for which I sent it.

I have spoken Scriptures over my own children's lives (unknown to them) and still continue to witness the promises of His word manifesting in their lives, and now, their children's lives. There is supernatural power in His word that is available to all of His children that many seem to be unaware of.

Although Ricky had this tough guy aura about him, he had a noticeable soft spot in his heart. At times, he let his guard down in a nonthreatening atmosphere. Over time he slowly opened his heart when he didn't feel judged or threatened emotionally and he began telling me about parts of his life that appeared to be unresolved. Without asking me directly he seemed to want my advice. I knew that to tell Ricky what to do in his personal circumstances could easily cross his line of defense and he may accuse me of calling him stupid as if he didn't think of that solution himself. So instead I would say, "Well, if I was in that situation these are some considerations I would think about doing." This would open up nonthreatening conversations where I could present some Godly wisdom for him to think about that might resolve some of his life's issues.

I was amazed a couple of days later when he was excited to tell me, "I did what you said and two of the things we talked about were settled." He was all excited and happy as if a ton of weight was lifted off his shoulders. Actually they were two trivial issues, but obviously he needed to talk it out with someone he began to trust.

Ricky had three children who were in their twenties, but he wasn't around much to raise them. The mother of the children divorced him and married someone else while he was in prison. He also had two younger children who were conceived in prison with an old girlfriend. She visited him during conjugal visits and she became his wife and lived with her mother as she waited for him to be released on parole. Eventually Ricky and his new wife and their two young children moved into his mother's house. Ricky's mother lived about 10 miles from my house.

Simple Faith Grows A Powerful Godly Warrior

One day I followed Ricky home with my pickup truck full of firewood he wanted that we removed from a job. I met his mother, his wife and his kids who were about four and five years old. His mother and his wife jokingly told me about Ricky's anger and rage issues, practically destroying many things he owned. They said if his electrical tools didn't work properly or if he made a mistake while using them, he would angrily break them in some way. A few times he kicked big dents into his car and even used a hammer and again a rock to break the side window in his anger. He also broke the front windshield twice in a rage.

I was looking at Ricky as they spoke about him and noticed he was nodding his head in agreement but he was embarrassed. His face was flushed and red. I responded and said, "Well, as long as he doesn't hit you guys!" They quickly responded saying, "Oh, no, we wouldn't stand for that." Then immediately Ricky's rage rose up. His anger snapped out in a flash as he declared, "If anyone ever touches one of my family, I'd kill them! I'll kill them dead!!"

We talked another fifteen minutes and his wife mentioned that Ricky spends most of his money fixing and replacing the things he breaks. It was hard for them to get ahead of their bills.

Ricky had been working with us for several months and I continued to speak uplifting Scriptures to him that seemed to fit the circumstances. He usually made a disgusting face and said, "Yeah, whatever..." as if he wasn't listening to me.

Although he was struggling to control his anger the other workers couldn't understand his snippiness and his negative comments. I challenged Ricky a few times a week over the next months by saying, "Whenever you are ready, Ricky, the Lord can remove that spirit of anger and rage from you and you'll be a new man, full of peace." His response would be, "Yeah right, I don't think so." I would answer and say, "I don't have to think so, because I know so. The Lord wants to reveal Himself to you and set you free." I told him that he had a calling on his life to set the captives free in his old home, the prison!

One day after work at my house I told Ricky I wanted to talk to him for a minute. I spoke to him face-to-face and shared a scenario with him. "Suppose someone walked up to you and said, 'Ricky, I think you and your mother are idiots!' Or, they may even say something worse, what would you say to them?" Ricky looked at me and said, "I wouldn't say anything to them. I would just knock them out so fast with my fist that if they're lucky they'd be waking up on the ground hours later." Then his anger was rising up as he thought about it and said, "Why? Did one of the guys working with us say something to you?" I quickly told him, "Not at all." Then I said, "What if I told you that you can say a prayer when you get up every morning that would quickly change your life? It will only take 15 to 20 seconds which I know you can handle once I explain and you understand the meaning of it. Ricky said, "Yeah right, the next thing you're going to tell me is that I have to go to church." I said, "No! In time you will want to go yourself without anyone twisting your arm." He said, "Yeah right, that will be the day!" A couple of days later I told Ricky to sit down on the picnic table behind my house as I went inside to get my Bible. I opened the Bible to Ephesians 6 and read verses 10 to 18 about putting on the full armor of God. I asked Ricky to listen as I read it. Then I had Ricky slowly read it out loud so he could hear the words with his own voice.

I clearly explained something that had never been explained or revealed to him before — how this Scripture related to what he was experiencing spiritually. I told him if he puts the full armor of God on every morning that within one month or less he'd have a peace he never experienced in his life. I told him now that he understands the scripture verses, I can share a shorter prayer version that he can speak or whisper out loud — it would only take 15 or 20 seconds privately in his bedroom. I gave him an example: "Father, in Jesus' name, I put on the full armor of God from the top of my head to the soles of my feet. I pick up the sword (your Word) and the shield (to protect me) and to extinguish the fiery darts of the enemy that comes against me. I plead the Blood of Jesus and Psalm 91 over me and my family."

Eventually in time I'll have you ask the Lord to put you in the spiritual front lines for battle in His army. I see you as a warrior, but right now you're spiritually on the wrong side. The victories you will experience and understand are when you stand on the other side!

Ricky listened intensely but I knew I was at the end of his attention span and didn't want to lose any ground I already obtained. So I quickly changed the subject and said that he did a great job today and then walked him to his car. That night I printed the 15 to 20 second prayer for him and I also wrote a simple salvation prayer that he can speak out in private before the Lord. Ricky's heart was like a rock. It was proud of his angry behavior that unexpectedly flared up concerning trivial issues. The results of the negative choices he had made in his life seemed to control him.

The next day after work I privately gave Ricky the prayers that I had written down for him. I challenged him again to put the full armor of God on every morning. I also explained the salvation prayer that he can speak out and receive the Lord Jesus Christ as his Lord and Savior.

Spiritual Life Goes From Rags to Riches – In Power

After that time I didn't speak another word related to my advice to him. About two weeks later after work, Ricky asked if he could talk to me about something. He seemed very concerned. He said, "Something weird is going on." My first immediate thought was that it's concerning his coworkers. But then he said that nothing seemed to bother him like it used to. And he felt like crying at times mainly when he watched certain movies. Then he said, "To tell you the truth, I've been crying for no reason at all like a weak sissy and I'm having a hard time dealing with it and trying to control it." As Ricky was speaking to me his eyes filled with tears. He seemed embarrassed and quickly turned to walk away with his head down wiping the tears that started flowing down his face with both hands. I smiled and said, "Hey, you've been saying that prayer we talked about, haven't you?"

Ricky leaned against one of my trucks with his back towards me trying to get his composure under control. I didn't want to walk towards him and make him feel more embarrassed, so I spoke to his back at a distance and I explained everything that was happening to him was a good thing.

Here's a summary of what I told him:

1. The Lord loves you and He is setting you free from the spiritual array of dark torment that's been following you around and operating through you for a long time.

2. You obviously asked the Lord to come into your heart and into your life to be your Lord and Savior by speaking out the Salvation Prayer: Parts 1 and 2 that I gave you.

3. The prayer you spoke renounced the father of lies and deception. It renounced the dominion of darkness and its cohorts who enticed you into anger, rage, and hate. It had even been unleashed toward yourself to a degree, but this had been disrupted in the past two weeks by you putting on the full armor of God every day.

4. Crying is a release of pain and emotional hurt that he had stuffed throughout his life, in combination with his spirit crying out, "Abba Father!" (Galatians 4:6).

5. A healing process had begun, so don't try to control it, but allow the Lord to continue His work in you.

6. Your tears will turn to joy and you'll feel happy for no reason. The Lord will give you a spirit of joy and you will experience peace beyond your understanding. It's written in Philippians 4:7 that the peace of God, which transcends all understanding, will guard your hearts and your mind in Christ Jesus. This also could be part of the crying that you are experiencing.

7. The Lord also gives us a spirit of adoption into the family of God (Romans 8:15). I told Ricky that I was excited for him! A new journey in his life had begun.

8. The old Ricky is passing away and the Lord is raising up a new Ricky — all things will become new to you! Don't fight it, although it is your choice to follow the Lord's leadings and His ways or continue down the same old path, the road you've been on.

9. The Lord will restore your conscience and will convict your heart concerning your past sins, bad behavior (stinking thinking) if you haven't surrendered those issues to Him yet. He is changing your heart of stone to a heart of flesh (Ezekiel 36:26).

I also told Ricky that one of the most important but very challenging issues that will hold him back from abundant life is holding unforgiveness in his heart toward anyone, including himself. It's written in Matthew 6:14 that if we don't forgive people who hurt or sinned against us in any degree, the Lord won't forgive us of our sins (which may be many). Sin also gives the enemy permission to torment and afflict us, even if we were the original victim of the sin or offense. I told Ricky to speak out to the Lord, again, not in his mind, but loud enough that he can hear his own voice. It's also important for the enemy to hear his confessions to the Lord because it breaks the power of any hold the enemy may have on him in that area. That's one reason why the enemy manifests itself upon a person in the attempt to stop the person from confessing their sins before the Lord. I told him to forgive anyone who comes to his thoughts. I reminded him, "Ask the Holy Spirit to reveal any other issues you may have buried in your heart or mind." I told Ricky to ask the Lord to fill those unforgiveness voids within him with the Heavenly Father's love. "The Heavenly Father's love will fill those empty void's and will start to crowd out other dark situations. Hidden darkness will be pushed up to the surface to be confessed or released. This process will continue until your heart is consumed in His love, that is, of course, if you accept it and allow it to happen. By being obedient to the Lord in this process you will accelerate your healing in areas possibly buried deep in your heart."

I continued to talk and encouraged Ricky not to fear this new journey. "The Lord has His hand on your shoulder and will never leave you or forsake you" (Hebrews 13:5). I told him to ask me or call me anytime he has questions about his new experiences or challenges and that I'll be there for him.

Ricky shrugged his shoulders and smiled as he walked to his car. He said, "Well, if any weirder things happen, I'll let you know," and he left to go home. The next few days it rained so we didn't work but on each of those rainy days Ricky called and wanted to meet me for lunch. He informed me that his family was noticing his calm behavior as he handled everyday issues. They all assumed he was troubled in some way and he would snap out of it eventually. He hadn't told his family about his new relationship with the Lord.

(continues in the next chapter)

NOTES

CHAPTER 23

A SLAVE TO DARKNESS TRANSFORMED INTO A GODLY SOLDIER

(PART 2 OF 4)

In this chapter:
- Believe In Your Heart That Love Moves Mountains
- The Impossible Becomes Possible in Christ!

Believe In Your Heart That Love Moves Mountains

A couple of days later Ricky said he spoke to his mother briefly about his Godly conversations with me. His mother informed him that a few years ago she went with some friends to a church revival meeting. The pastor prayed for her twice that night and she was told by her friends that she immediately collapsed to the floor when the pastor touched her on both occasions that night. She told Ricky she didn't remember falling and that she didn't feel any different afterwards. I explained that sometimes the enemy causes a person to "blackout" and fall. This abruptly blocks them from receiving an experiential touch or blessing from the Lord. (*I explained this in an earlier story.*) So I invited myself to go see his mother. I convinced Ricky we should go together that afternoon to his mother's house, where Ricky and his family lives, and pray for her and see what happens.

Later when we arrived at Ricky's house his mother was home alone because his wife and kids were at the store. I had a short conversation with his mother and she gave me permission to pray for her, but only if she was seated in a chair in her kitchen. Because of her last embarrassing reaction in front of her friends, she was very reluctant to surrender to the Holy Spirit and wanted to stay in alerted control.

I spoke blessings over her life and then decided it was time to pray for Ricky. He was standing between the kitchen counter top and the kitchen table. His mother was still sitting in the chair. I said, "Okay, Ricky, it's your turn. Ricky started to make excuses about not needing prayer." But I said, "Be quiet and give me your hands and repeat after me." He repeated the salvation prayer — part one and part two again. Then I told him to close his eyes and put his heart on the Lord. I placed my hand on his head and asked the Holy Spirit to come upon him in power. Ricky had a smile on his face as he stood with his arms out in front of him with open hands to receive from the Lord. As I spoke blessings and Scriptures over him, I was also breaking the power of certain iniquities and works of the enemy over his life. His body started to tremble and his smile disappeared as his mouth opened and his arms lowered slowly to his side as I was speaking over Him. He looked like he was in a drunken stupor. He eventually put one arm around my shoulder as he slowly started to collapse resting most of his weight on me. I noticed his knees started to bend, so I quickly pushed one of my knees against his knee, locking it in a straight position to keep him from collapsing.

Then I wrapped my arms around him to hold him up. Most of his weight was leaning on me at this point. I continued to speak over him through the whole ordeal. I promised him that I wouldn't let him fall on the floor which resolved one of his concerns before we prayed. In a low soft voice, he spoke, "I have to sit down." His mother brought a chair over to him, but I had to hold his whole-body weight as I released his knee that I had locked so I could quickly turn his body and place him on the chair. Ricky's mother said, "He acts and looks totally drugged." I smiled and said, "He is totally drunk on the new Holy Spirit wine." Ricky was barely able to speak but said in a low voice, "I have to go lay down." His mother and I were supporting him in his chair, so I told him that he needed to wait a while until he could support himself before he tried to walk to his bedroom. About 20 minutes later, he walked very slowly to his bedroom door as I supported him. He said that he would call me later which he never did. I left his house about 3 PM and didn't see him again until the next morning at work. When he arrived at work he was totally smiling with a big grin on his face. He started to tell me about his experience and he didn't seem to care about the other guys listening. He told me that when he laid on his back on his bed after I left yesterday, he felt this tingling throughout most of his body. Then all of a sudden he felt as if his body was floating higher and higher off his bed. He said, "I had a peace at the same time I felt the fear of the floating sensation. Then I remembered what you said about fear, that it is a spirit and that I can rebuke it and command it to go away! Which I did in Jesus name. I asked Jesus to put me back on my bed. Suddenly I felt myself floating back down onto my bed. I heard my wife calling me in a low voice, as if she was far away talking through the end of a 20-foot funnel. I kept hearing her speak, "Ricky, Ricky, can you hear me? Ricky, are you alright? Ricky, wake up!"

He said, "Then she pushed me and then I heard her screaming my name. I asked her, "Why are you screaming at me? I'm right here!" She said I wouldn't wake up. She thought something was wrong with me. Ricky said his wife woke him up around 6 PM which was really weird to him because he thought I left his house only 30 minutes earlier. He explained that he was awake the whole time experiencing intense tingle and slight vibration throughout his inner body. Eventually it led to a feeling of floating higher and higher out of his bed.

Ricky looked at me and said, how can three hours of time feel like 30 minutes?! I told Ricky that he was caught up in the spirit and the Lord was visiting him there. In the spirit, time does not exist as we know it. There is no time in the spirit, time is eternity. According to 2 Peter 3:8, one day in heaven is like a thousand years on earth. *More on that...in another story.*

The Impossible Becomes Possible in Christ!

Later that day the other guys (workers) privately asked me what was going on with Ricky. They said he was making jokes about himself and laughing a lot concerning trivial things. They thought he was acting very strange and actually smiling a lot. They were waiting for his angry attitude to pop up. But it never did. They wanted to know what I said to him and what he was so happy about. I challenged them to ask Ricky themselves why he was so happy. I had to laugh a few times myself as I listened to his happy attitude change as he delighted in himself and the workers around him. The Lord really set him free yesterday afternoon from the demonic spiritual torment and stronghold that he unknowingly allowed to traffic with him for years.

I was surprised that one of the workers in the group spoke up and asked Ricky, "Why are you so happy today?" What surprised me more was Ricky's immediate smiling response, "Jesus set me free yesterday and I feel totally different." Then Ricky advised them that they too should repent and ask Jesus to be their Lord and Savior. He said, "Jesus would change your life, too!" Then he started to tell them about some of his experiential encounters he was having with the Lord. Ricky was excited and smiling as he told them his testimony.

He looked over to me at times for affirmations as he spoke. I would respond by saying, "That's right. He's telling you the truth!" As I stood there listening and watching Ricky, I had to smile as I thought Ricky had become an evangelist overnight as he revealed his testimony to them while not cursing at all. "And they overcame him by the blood of the Lamb, and by the word of their testimony; and they loved not their lives unto the death" (Revelation 12:11).

When it was time to go home Ricky offered to buy me an early dinner because he wanted me to explain in more detail why he felt so different. I spent about two hours with him explaining everything. The Lord spoke to his heart, filling him to overflowing with truth and wonders Ricky couldn't receive earlier. Part of Ricky's heart was now like a dry sponge soaking up the Heavenly Father's love he never experienced or heard about before. When we left the diner, Ricky was on fire and hungry for another touch from the Lord. He became very teachable and was starting to discern and understand answers to questions in his mind before he ever asked them. I told him the Lord hears all his thoughts and is answering his questions like it says in John 10:27, "My sheep listen to my voice; I know them and they follow me." I encouraged him to catch this revelation in his heart and know the sound of His voice, because He's always speaking.

Many Christians believe a lie by saying that they can't hear the Lord's voice or that He never speaks to them. This hurts the Lord's heart because He loves to commune with us not only in His word, but personally and intimately in all our circumstances. He wants to fill and consume our hearts with His love. Walking in unbelief shuts out hearing His voice. The enemy tries to keep us believing that way. That's why so many people are deceived. They are hearing the voice of the enemy as he deceitfully leads them away from the heart of God, distracting them from knowing and experiencing the love that their Heavenly Father has for them. The spiritual battleground between the one true God and Satan IS YOUR HEART!

If you have been walking in unbelief concerning hearing the Lord's voice, it is easy to rectify. Ask the Lord to forgive your past unbelief and surrounding circumstances that held you back. Agree in your heart that you are not the exception of not hearing His voice (which is what the enemy speaks to you) if you are one of His sheep (belonging to Him). Ask the Holy Spirit who is our teacher and comforter to spiritually tune your heart, your ears, and your mind to the frequency of His voice so you can discern it clearly.

A week earlier Ricky asked, "How will I know it's the Lord's voice speaking to me?" I gave him an easy exercise and knew it would help him quickly discern whose voice is speaking to him in his thoughts. I explained, "There are three voices we hear. One is the Lord's voice. Another is your own voice. The third is the enemy's voice."

I told him to bring all his thoughts captive and make them obedient to Jesus Christ (2 Corinthians 10:5). I encouraged him to start examining all of his current thoughts and identify which of the three voices is speaking. I said, "Ricky, with a little practice you will definitely distinguish which voice is speaking to you. It's important to remember that the enemy can NOT read your mind or hear your thoughts. Jesus knows everything about you including all your secrets. He can also hear and know your thoughts."

In the next chapter, I explain to Ricky the importance of recognizing the three main voices that speak to our thoughts among other things. He has to understand which voice is speaking and identify the origin. This is a life changing exercise for anyone.

(continues in the next chapter)

NOTES

CHAPTER 24

IDENTIFY THE THREE VOICES SPEAKING TO YOU

(PART 3 OF 4)

In this chapter:
- Three Voices
- Defeating the Enemy's Deception

Three Voices

There are three main voices that speak to you. Which one are you listening to?

1. The Voice of The Lord

2. Your Personal Inner Voice (thoughts)

3. The Enemy's Voice (negative thoughts)

It's very important to recognize what voice Is speaking to your thoughts. It Is life changing!!!

I know when Ricky understands this truthful revelation, he'll recognize he has been captivated and victimized by the negative torment of the kingdom of darkness. Because of his recent spiritual experiences, his heart and mind are wide open for a change in life.

1. The Voice of the Lord – There is no condemnation in Christ Jesus (Romans 8:1). Jesus loves you so much that he died for your sins so that you can have eternal life with Him and our Heavenly Father.
   - He desires a deep relationship with you.
   - He convicts your heart in love and not condemnation when you sin.
   - He gives you Godly wisdom liberally to resolve your issues (James 1:5-6).
   - He will only speak good words concerning you.
   - He does not judge you in your thoughts.
   - He affirms you and your best interest.
   - He lifts you up.

- His word is true and consistent concerning you.
- He doesn't love one person more than another.
- He is no respecter of people or positions (Acts 10:33, Romans 2:11).
- His voice is caring and peaceful (John 14:27).
- He will never leave you or forsake you (Deuteronomy 31:6).
- He sticks closer to you then a brother (Proverbs 18:24)

2. Your Personal Inner Voice (Thoughts)
   - Your voice could be positive (good) or negative (bad) concerning yourself or others.
   - It contains many of your life's experiences, memories and emotions from childhood through adulthood — positive, negative, confused, or judgmental.
   - It holds thoughts concerning your beliefs and values.
   - Negative and positive words you received concerning yourself which can be rectified through healing and understanding.
   - It holds emotional attitudes and biases

3. The Enemy's Voice
   - It always speaks negative deceptive words and thoughts concerning yourself and others.
   - It is never uplifting unless It's trying to seduce you into sin.
   - It makes you feel like a failure to the point where you stop trying.
   - It makes you put off doing something so that it never gets done.

It's important to remember that the enemy hates you because you are a child of God. And It hates God for throwing It and its cohorts out of heaven. Its only mission is to steal, kill and destroy (John 10:10). If It could, It would destroy your entire life. It does not respect you in Its words and thoughts that It speaks to your mind.

I told Ricky that you should never play a mind game with the enemy, because you will always lose. Most people don't realize their negative thoughts concerning themselves or others can be spoken from the enemy's mouth, to their thoughts, possibly taking root in their mind as truth. Unfortunately, many people open their lives to the enemy by sinning which could have tragic consequences, if repentance is not offered to the Lord. For example: Practicing witchcraft or being involved in the occult will definitely add to the negative voices, some may be heard audibly. The enemy attempts to deceive everyone who will listen to "It" in their thoughts and feelings, including their emotions. It can trigger people's hidden negative emotions extensively that may be attached to stuffed unhealed past hurts or trauma as spoken in previous ministry situations.

It's very important to recognize the enemy's voice so you can ignore the lies and deny It power or influence in your life. If you believe what the enemy speaks, it will only drag you down a rabbit hole of more lies and deception. It enjoys watching you condemn yourself and others. This is a problem of epidemic proportions for people of all ages who use anti-depressants and other meds to cope with emotional issues such as depression, low self-esteem, or anxiety. The enemy's overwhelming tactics is convincing many in their thoughts to ISOLATE themselves from everybody, so that it can bombard you with constant negative lies about yourself and your conditions. Unfortunately, the rabbit hole can lead to addictions which could lead to even worse conditions than the depression or anxiety. It is written in Ephesians 6:12, "For our struggle is not against flesh and blood, but against the rulers, against the authorities, against the powers of this dark world and against the spiritual forces of evil in the heavenly realms."

One easy and understandable way to discern which voice you are hearing is to review your thoughts as you receive them. Our minds are full of thoughts most of the time. Positive or happy thoughts make us smile and feel good about ourselves and our life. Negative or sad thoughts have the opposite effect.

Take a couple of minutes and ask these questions. Where did that thought come from? Was it positive or negative?

If it was positive, again, where did it come from? Was I thinking about something that led me to this happy thought? For example, did I recently receive a gift, promotion, good report, or a kind note from a friend earlier that day? If you can't think of a practical reason that prompted the happy thought or emotions, then it likely came from the Lord – Voice #1.

The Lord's voice is often heard in our thoughts and heart. He speaks to us all the time, but most people don't know that or are unaware of it. Unfortunately, many of His sheep who received Him as Lord and Savior don't recognize His voice. Some believe the enemy's lie that they can't hear His voice or He's not speaking to them at all. John 10: 27-28 says, my sheep listen to my voice; I know them, and they follow me. I give them eternal life, and they shall never perish; no one will snatch them out of my hand.

If your thoughts are negative about yourself or someone else, follow the same process to identify the source. A negative thought can be a little harder to discern where it came from at first. Eventually it becomes easier and even fun as you learn to identify which voice is speaking to you and it gives you the ability to overcome the enemy and have a peaceful mind and life. Remember, the more you practice, the more natural it will become. Soon, it will take only moments to discern the voice speaking.

Remember, we live in a spiritual world of darkness and light and the Bible says that is where the real battle exists.

Discerning where a negative thought comes from involves learning the difference between #2 - your voice, and #3 - the enemy's voice. When the Lord showed me this exercise, I was amazed at how often the enemy spoke negative thoughts into my mind that I believed were my own. Negative thoughts only originate from our own voice or the enemy's voice, #2 or #3.

So, again, if you have a negative thought or feeling about yourself or someone else or any negative thoughts, or beliefs in general pops-up, ask the following questions:

1. Where did that negative thought come from?
2. Was I just thinking about something that brought it up?

If a negative thought doesn't pertain to something I was currently thinking about, or just pops up for no reason, then it was the enemy's voice speaking to you, #3. This happens more than you think and most people are tormented by a barrage of negative thoughts that come from the enemy's voice. Over time people actually start to believe these thoughts are their own and that the lies are actually the truth concerning themselves or someone else. The lies become their reality and mood. They will adjust their attitude to the false thoughts that they believe are true. This negatively starts to influence their entire life and those around them. Over time, this can cause depression, confusion, anxiety, less friends, and more. Many people seek relief from doctors who are quick to label them with a negative diagnosis and prescribe Rx medications to "help." It is very sad because they don't realize why this is happening to them. The enemy loves it because he hates you and wants to keep you from your purpose and destiny in the Lord. The enemy tries to keep you from a relationship with God, blaming God for your hurts, disappointments, and problems by persistently speaking these lies to your thoughts until you believe them. This strategy can keep you from knowing and experiencing the love of God.

I told Ricky the enemy robbed his true destiny for most of his life. Half of his life was wasted in prison, but his mind was infiltrated and demonically controlled and imprisoned much longer than that. I encouraged him to remember as a born-again Christian he's a child of God and his eternal destiny is in Heaven. The enemy's destiny is in the lake of fire or Hell (Revelation 20:10) and he can't change that. A long time ago the enemy, Lucifer, now Satan, was in charge of praise and worship in Heaven where he lived and experienced all the blessings of God. Lucifer was originally created by God for this purpose (Ezekiel 28 :12-19) and lived in the presence and glory of God. He knew God face-to-face but became jealous of the praise and worship that was given to God in heaven because he wanted it for himself. In short, Lucifer rebelled against God. There was a battle in heaven resulting in Lucifer and many angles that followed him to be cast out of heaven to earth by God and condemned to hell (Isaiah 14:12-15, Revelation 12:7-9). Contrary to many people's beliefs, Lucifer or Satan, is not in hell yet. 1 Peter 5:8 says,"Be alert and of sober mind. Your enemy the devil prowls around like a roaring lion looking for someone to devour." Satan will be thrown into hell on judgment day along with many others who were deceived by Satan to live a sinful rebellious life. It is written that the penalty for sin is death which is the second death or eternity in hell (separation from God) forever (Revelation 21:8).

I continued to speak and reveal the truth to Ricky concerning the goals and tactics the enemy operates through called deception.

The Good News is that Jesus Christ is our redeemer and savior (Ephesians 1:7). He died for us. He took our sins upon Himself, so all who believe and receive Him as their Lord and Savior will be saved, receiving a free gift of eternal life with Him in heaven. That is why Satan hates us. He cannot contend with God or hurt Him. But he can hurt God's heart as he tempts and deceives the children of God into sin, possibly causing them to be separated from God for eternity. Satan will look for ways for them to go to hell with him. If Satan can't deceive you and gain your soul, he will torment you if he can. Use wisdom and stay away from the clutches of sin he presents to you. We must avoid him. Stay out of his camp. Satan and the fallen angels were sent to earth and live and exists in the spirit known as the spiritual world which exists in this world all around us. Although they are bound to an extent, they have freedom to tempt and deceive. Satan is evil and only wants to steal, kill and destroy.

It's important to mention not all of our negative thoughts are from the enemy. Often, your own VOICE #2 is to blame. See, we all have negative experiences, loss, arguments, negative words spoken to us throughout our lives. We often connect past negative experiences to our current thoughts and attitudes without even being aware of them. In order to break the cycle and power of negative thoughts based on past experiences, ask the Lord, to show you whom you need to forgive (including yourself) for past offenses against you, things that you have harbored in your heart. You can be released from every circumstance. Give it all to Jesus with a forgiving heart. Let Him release you. He'll heal your mind, body, soul, and spirit.

Defeating the Enemy's Deception

How can we defeat the enemy's deception and negative comments he says about you and the thoughts that he brings? Remember the enemy is the father of lies. Once you start to recognize the enemy's voice and destructive lying statements, do the following: Speak out loud enough to the Lord and thank Him for the opposite TRUTH concerning you, the opposite of what the enemy is speaking in your thoughts.

For example, the enemy cannot read your mind or hear your thoughts, but the Lord can. A thought may pop up, "Nobody loves me and I'm all alone." If you receive that thought as your own, and believe it, you give it power and permission to work in your mind and heart in your life. The enemy will speak it repeatedly to your mind. It will echo in your thoughts possibly convincing you that the thought is true. Don't be deceived. Do not believe it! If you actually feel unloved or alone, it may have started with the enemy continually speaking this deception to you!

Once you recognize the enemy's voice, immediately resist and cast down any thoughts by speaking out (proclaiming) the truth or the opposite to the Lord. In this example you could say, "Thank you, Lord Jesus, for loving me. You love me so much that you died for my sins. I am never alone because it is written that you will never leave me nor forsake me, (Hebrews 13:5) (Deuteronomy 31:6) and I know you cannot deny your own word" (2 Timothy 2:13).

As you speak out the TRUTH and hear your own voice proclaim it, the negative thought immediately loses its power and leaves your mind, your spoken proclamation of truth replaces the lie. When the enemy hears the truth you spoke to the Lord, it defeats him (the enemy) and that lie concerning you. You don't need to fight with the enemy directly because declaring the Lord's truth or His word over you is more powerful and peaceful than arguing with the enemy over a lie. John 8:32 says, "then you will know the truth, and the truth will set you free."

Continually battling with the enemy (trying to convince him, or yourself) concerning your thought-life only makes you exhausted. You want to live in peace and feel good about yourself. Remember, the enemy loves to torment you. Don't let him pull you into his games. Just speak the truth out how Jesus sees you!

As you begin to recognize the voices or thoughts and identify who is speaking, you can disregard the spoken thoughts of the enemy and have peace of mind.

"Submit yourselves, then, to God. Resist the devil, and he will flee from you" (James 4:7).

After so many years of receiving and hearing the enemy's indoctrination of deceptive lies, you may wholeheartedly believe everything the enemy has spoken to you about yourself. So, when you speak out the opposite truth to the Lord you may feel like you are lying to yourself and to God. But continue to speak out the truth even when you are feeling uncomfortable. As you hear your own words spoken, that real truth spoken out will take root in your heart. Continue repeating that truth to the Lord and listen to your own voice speaking it. Shortly you will begin to own it and you'll believe the real truth about yourself. The Lord will begin restoring you as you believe His truth concerning you. The next time the enemy's voice speaks, you'll discern it as a lie spoken from the enemy (almost immediately) and you will NOT receive it. Remember you are wonderfully created by God and made in His image (Genesis 1:27).

There are other ways to deal with this issue. You can rebuke the enemy and command him to be silent, which may work temporally. You can confront the enemy on the issues. The Lord has shown me these truths to be most effective in bringing healing, peace, victory, and understanding. It doesn't take long. The freedom and the understanding of the truth spoken out by you in response to the known deceptive thoughts you heard, develops a heart and mind of true peace in a short period of time.

I explained to Ricky in depth the importance of being able to discern which of the three voices was speaking to his mind. He realized he had been listening faithfully and reacting to the voice of the enemy. He confessed that most of his life he'd been angry because of the rotten hand he felt he was dealt. He said he had to fight to keep anything good in his life. But now the Lord (Holy Spirit) has removed the black cloud he was engulfed and living in. The Lord was changing his life from the thoughts of being defeated and hopeless into gaining a new sense of accomplishment and hope for the future. The Lord was sanctifying and setting him free!

(continues in the next chapter)

NOTES

CHAPTER 25

JESUS' PRESENCE EXPOSES SPIRITUAL DARKNESS AROUND RICKY

(PART 4 OF 4)

In the chapter:
- The Light of Jesus' Presence in Us Causes Darkness to Manifest
- Understanding the Enemy's Tactics and Know Your Prayer Strategies
- In Jesus We Are Victorious in Spiritual Battle

The Light of Jesus' Presence in Us Causes Darkness to Manifest

Ricky approached me a week later after work and wanted to talk about a problem he was having at home. He told me his wife had been angry and yelling at him almost all week. "I don't understand why she's so angry. So now I'm yelling back at her to tell me what's wrong. She brings up little stupid things that I've always done, but they were never a big deal before." He said, "For the last two nights she can't spend the entire night in bed with me because for some reason she doesn't want to be that close to me anymore. If it gets much worse, I'm afraid she's going to want a divorce, because it's that bad!" He didn't understand what to do. She had never acted like this before.

As I thought about it, I started to smile. Ricky looked at me puzzled and asked, "Why are you smiling? This is a serious problem!" I looked at him and asked, "You really don't know why this is happening?" He said, "If I knew what the issue was, I wouldn't be standing here talking to you about it!"

I told him that he came a long way in a short amount of time restoring his relationship with the Lord. I said, "The Lord has set you free in many areas of your life." He had been praying and seeking the Lord with all his heart and was developing an intimate relationship with Him in his prayer closet, the secret place. It was obvious he was a changed man.

I explained that what was happening with his wife was more her issue than his although it was affecting them both. I told Ricky that as a result of surrendering his life to the Lord and growing in intimacy with Him, the Lord's light was increasing and becoming brighter in him. The light of Jesus was radiating through him making him a brighter shining one in the spirit realm. I explained further that the Lord's radiant light in him now exposes and uncovers the hidden darkness in your wife (and others, as the Lord uses him). "The darkness in her hates your guts" and, of course, she doesn't understand or know why she's so angry. Also, she doesn't realize the anger she's experiencing is actually the enemy's anger toward you because of the Lord's presence emanating through you. She is blaming you to justify her angry feelings and behavior.

Understanding the Enemy's Tactics and Know Your Prayer Strategies

Sometimes the enemy attaches itself to prior hurts or traumas, disappointment or abandonment emotions in a person's life. If these past issues are left unresolved or unhealed, they may become triggered by the enemy's deceptive secret attacks, giving the person a reason to be emotionally upset or angry, but usually for no apparent substantial reason. The enemy and his cohorts can be attached to some negative emotions or hurt that we "sucked up" and stuffed down to our lower belly. This gave us the ability to move forward in life and deal with the issues later. This is a reason why the enemy stays hidden and undetected unless the Lord's light shines on it. Then the enemy will manifest and reveal itself, but most people are unaware of the cause and don't recognize the spiritual enemy or its potential destructive work in a relationship or a "single" person's life with different types of relational parameters.

I told Ricky that it's easy to resolve the issue when you discern the cause of the problem. Ricky's wife was a practicing member of a mainline religious church that spoke shallow Godly messages and didn't teach much on developing an intimate relationship with the Lord. Before I met Ricky, he had no relationship with the Lord. His wife was the spiritual head of the household. I told Ricky that the enemy is involved in spiritual warfare causing a division between him and his wife. I told him, "You have to confront the enemy in this circumstance." Most Christians are unaware of this successful spiritual strategy. Ricky was a little nervous about that and wanted me to confront his wife for him. I encouraged Ricky saying, "It's fun and very easy. Besides, the battle is not yours but the Lord's" (2 Chronicles 20:15).

The enemy is not creative with its schemes. It works to create havoc (in this case, in Ricky's marriage) with Its deceptive strategies. You must discern the most effective prayer strategy for the battle the enemy is confronting you with. The Holy Spirit will lead you to all truth if you ask Him and He will show or teach you how to pray effectively against the enemy's attack in each case. Sometimes we need to confess any sin we may be harboring. We may need to release someone from sins committed against us. We must be free from the grip of unforgiveness even if we feel they don't deserve it.

Ricky thought about it for a moment then took a deep breath and responded, "Okay, tell me what to say or do."

I told him, here are some steps to take when your wife goes to sleep tonight:

1. Ask the Lord to forgive you for all your sins and for not taking your rightful place as the spiritual head of your household. Biblically, the order of authority is God, man then woman. Many households are out of order for various reasons (Corinthians 11:3).

2. (Speak or whisper out) I command all the darkness and their cohorts who are speaking to my wife or constructing any negative plans concerning me and my family to hear what I speak right now in the name of Jesus Christ of Nazareth and I rebuke any disobedience. *Remember! The FULL authority of Christ is in you. Ask that His voice be heard in the spirit realm, through you, causing darkness to tremble, scream and run away. Darkness HAS to obey your command, and all addressed are listening. Catch this TRUTH in your HEART and OWN IT!!! EXPECT, EXPECT, EXPECT!!*

3. Then speak or whisper out, "I take back all spiritual authority over this house and my family that I relinquished to my wife during my years of absence in Jesus' name."

4. Gently put your hand on her and whisper under your breath (so that she can't hear you) with righteous assertiveness, "In the name of Jesus Christ of Nazareth, I break the power and plans of all darkness and their cohorts that are coming against me, my wife, and this household. I command all of your plans to be null and void in Jesus' name! I plead the blood of Jesus over all of it and I ask Jesus to wash it all away."

5. Then command all the darkness to leave your wife and family and go directly to Jesus for Him to deal with.

6. Then ask the Holy Spirit to come and fill all voids in your wife (including yourself) with the love of Father God, in Jesus name.

7. Speak or whisper out and bless your house. Dedicate it and all its contents to Jesus Christ. Bless the air and dedicate the continual air in the house to Jesus Christ of Nazareth. Ask the Lord's presence to spiritually light up the air in your house. And believe it!! Remember, the enemy is called the prince

of the air. THEY WON'T HANG AROUND IN HIS LIGHT.

8. Command all open doors in the spirit pertaining to you and your family, the house, to be closed, sealing them with the blood of Jesus. Ask Jesus to summon a Captain Warrior Angel to be at my house and around my family night and day to do all spiritual battle

I told Ricky, "This sequence of prayers will definitely work and it may also give you some confidence. You can ask the Holy Spirit for help to know how to pray effectively, if you forget what I spoke to you." We discussed this prayer strategy Friday afternoon before Ricky went home from work.

I thought about the possible results of his prayers often throughout the weekend, but when Ricky came in on Monday to work, I forgot to ask him about the results of his prayers that weekend for his wife. Then on Tuesday morning I asked him as soon as he arrived. "Hey Ricky," I said, "Did you get a chance to pray for your wife during the weekend?" He smiled and said with excitement, "Oh, yeah, I forgot to call you. It was really cool. I waited for her to fall asleep. Then I asked the Lord for forgiveness and whispered out that I'm back and taking back all my spiritual authority, as the man of the household. I didn't remember everything you told me, so I asked the Holy Spirit to help me. I placed my hand softly on her and quietly commanded all the demons, all the darkness, to leave, in Jesus name."

In Jesus We Are Victorious In Spiritual Battle

"She started moaning then suddenly screamed and quickly sat up in the bed," he continued. "And I acted as if I was sleeping and mumbled, what's going on with you?" She told him that she must have had a bad nightmare. Ricky was amazed at what happened and told his wife that he just prayed for her and that a bunch of darkness left fast making her scream and sit up. Ricky said, "Of course, she didn't believe me and responded, "'Yeah, right!'". Her spoken response reminded me of Ricky's past responses to me.

Ricky said he waited until she went back to sleep and softly placed his hand back on her and continued to whisper prayers. He said she started to moan and move a little but didn't scream or jump up again. He said that Saturday and Sunday were the best times they spent together since he returned home, "She didn't yell and act angry at me the whole weekend!"

When he confronted her about the week of hell they had been experiencing, she couldn't point to the reasons of her anger towards him. Ricky said it was hard to believe the immediate positive change in their relationship that weekend because of a short prayer. So, then he was excited to pray for his brother's marriage problems thinking darkness may be interfering with their troubles also.

About three months later, Ricky was arrested for parole violations and was sent back to prison to finish his term. He was released four months later on good behavior completing his prison time. He was finally free owing no more prison time.

While Ricky was in prison for those four months, he called me collect a few times to ask me about manifestations he was experiencing as he prayed and laid hands-on other inmates. He was excited about what was happening and needed advice on how to handle certain dark manifesting situations. He told me that many of the inmates were afraid of him and did not want him touching them because of what they were witnessing. Ricky started going to church there in prison. It was held twice a month. He attended a Bible class there also for those four months of his incarceration. The pastor that led prison-church and bible classes was amazed at his spiritual gifts and encouraged him. Ricky told the pastor that his boss prayed an impartation of the Holy Spirit over him. He said, "The pastor was a nice person but couldn't help to fully answer questions concerning spiritual manifestations or explain how to get a person free of issues that we use to talk about."

Ricky operated out of simple faith and truth he learned believing that the Lord has already defeated the enemy at the cross. But many times the enemy has to be reminded of that fact. The Lord used Ricky to cast off the destructive darkness and set the captives free spiritually, emotionally, and physically in the prison. He said it was changing their lives forever right in front of him.

Ricky and I prayed for many members of his family who experienced all kinds of cool, powerful manifestations which also made a huge impact in their lives and the lives of their friends.

Ricky worked with me for a few months after his final release. Eventually, he and his family moved away to avoid his past criminal friend's influence. He started a new life with his family and his new friend, teacher and savior, Jesus Christ.

NOTES

CHAPTER 26

KAREN UNKNOWINGLY INTERACTS WITH A REAPER DEMON

(PART 1 OF 2)

In this chapter:
- Karen Unknowingly Invites a Dark Spirit to Live In Her House
- The Lord Reveals Dark Spirits Attachment to Physical Objects

One day we were ministering to a lady named Betty who is in her 70's. She was harboring deep unforgiveness issues concerning her recently deceased husband of 50 years. As we were discussing her questions concerning the physical realm and the spiritual realm, she began showing concern for her daughter who was in her 40's at the time. She said her daughter called her a day ago about some recent spiritual encounters. Karen, her daughter, mentioned she was alarmed that she heard somebody whisper her own name in her ear. Betty said she was unsure of the facts that brought the strange phenomena into her daughter's house but wanted to know if we could meet with her daughter if she agreed. Three days later Betty's daughter called and set up an 11 AM appointment that week. When we arrived Betty was there to introduce us to Karen who seemed to be an outgoing and engaging person. Karen sat down with us and told us when these spiritual encounters began. She had been dating Bubba for six months when they both decided he should move into her house. It would be more convenient for them and they would share the house expenses saving them money. Although we never met Bubba, she said he became a little controlling since he moved in with her three months ago. She said Bubba was a nice guy though.

Karen Unknowingly Invites a Dark Spirit to Live In Her House

Karen mentioned that Bubba didn't have much furniture, but he cherished and seemed to protect a piece of framed metal artwork that they hung on the wall in the dining room. "She said that Bubba's grandmother made it when she was in her 20s and she gave it to Bubba when he was 15 years old to be a remembrance of her after her passing (sometime in the future). She said, "Bubba was in his 40s now. His grandmother has been dead for years. Since she died, he always felt her presence and believed that her spirit was attached to the framed metal artwork that she gave him. That's why we hung it in the dining room so that she could be close to us."

Although I believed differently than Karen and I recognized the deception, I didn't want to be rude and decided to listen to her complete story before I responded. Karen said that she also felt as if his grandmother was staring at her at times. She said, "It felt creepy at first but now I'm used to her. For the last few months since Bubba moved in, she has been following me around the house. I can feel her behind me when I'm cooking, doing the dishes, and even when I'm in the bathroom. I'm always talking to her and sometimes I ask, 'Is that you, grandma, standing behind me?' Then suddenly I can feel the hairs on the back of my neck go up. Sometimes I get a slight chill as she confirms her presence."

She was telling us everything. She said, "Although I speak to her a lot, I never heard her speak back to me until last week. While I was in the kitchen doing the dishes, I could feel her standing behind me as usual, but then I heard her speak my name in my left ear very slowly and clearly in a low voice. It felt creepy and scared me a little at first because I wasn't expecting it. I got a chill and the hairs on the back of my neck felt like they were standing up again. I quickly moved away from the sink and called Bubba to tell him that his grandmother just audibly said my name in my left ear." Bubba didn't believe me because she never spoke to him audibly. He said my mind was playing games on me, but I knew the voice was not spoken in my mind. It was audible in my ear and it was spoken from the outside of me."

I thought intensely about it all as she was speaking and she added, "I don't know if it was a woman's voice or a man's voice. It was just a voice!" Karen said that it was really strange when Bubba came home from work that day angry. "He was angry that I was speaking to his grandmother. He'd been hearing me for the last three months once I recognized her presence in my house. Bubba scolded me as if I was a child, telling me to never speak to his grandmother again. Well, that didn't go over well with me. We fought about it for two days before we both calmed down."

Karen said she didn't know what to do from that point concerning her relationship with his grandmother's spirit. She didn't want his grandmother to feel that she was being rejected. Then Karen smiled and asked me, "What do you think about the situation?" (Isaiah 8:19).

At this moment Karen's mother, Betty, stood up and said, "I have to leave. I can't deal with this stuff." Her facial expression revealed her shock and unbelief as she listened to her daughter's story. She even apologized for having us come out and waste our time. But I told Betty we were not wasting our time. There is a real spiritual issue that is happening here and we can help Karen by giving her some suggestions. Betty rolled her eyes in unbelief and walked out the door.

We have worked with people numerous times in similar and worse scenarios. I knew Karen and Bubba's situation could get worse if they continued to walk and live in this spiritual deception. I want to reiterate a point that I spoke of in many experiential stories. The enemy is not creative in the deception or games it plays in people's lives. The deceptions vary slightly in degree depending on the circumstances, but the victims are always different. At times the Lord uses us to warn the blind-sighted or to warn potential victims from walking into a trap of spiritual darkness which usually manifests itself some way in the person's life. Demonic permission enhances the enemy's purpose to steal, kill, and destroy the lives of the children of God in many different areas of their life, if It can.

In more than thirty years of spiritual encounters, the Lord continues to give us divine appointments. He leads the ministry. He teaches us and reveals the enemy's hidden agendas. The Lord's light of His presence in us exposes darkness and causes it to manifest. Jesus Christ has authority over all spiritual entities. They must obey when He speaks and commands through us.

Again, the mainline church is asleep and does not preach, teach or release the children of God in this area. They do not encourage Christ in them to set the captives free. This is one reason why the enemy is having a heyday with many members of the Church and it grieves the Lord's heart.

After Karen's mother left, we prayed and asked the Holy Spirit to open Karen's heart and mind to receive what we were going to explain to her as the Lord leads. We spoke out and commanded all present darkness in the house to stand at attention and not to move in Jesus' name. We broke its power while pleading the Blood of Jesus Christ of Nazareth over the eyes and ears of the enemy from seeing or hearing any of our conversation with Karen, in Jesus name. This short prayer command prevents the enemy from hearing or seeing our conversation including any prayer strategy that we may discuss with Karen. It usually prevents the enemy from manifesting or speaking to the persons thoughts creating fear as if we are the enemy, causing the ministry to stop and possibly requesting that we leave their house.

The Lord Reveals Dark Spirit Attachments to Physical Objects

I asked Karen to listen to us for ten minutes so we could explain what was going on concerning the spirit she invited into her house. I told her that she could ask all the questions she wanted after that. She agreed to this. I explained that the spirit in her house is not Bubba's grandmother. It is a dark spirit that somehow was attached to the grandmother's artwork knowingly or unknowingly. I went on, "The longer you allow it to stay, the bolder it will become because you are giving it permission to stay. This spirit is not your friend. In fact, it hates you. In time, it may even invite other dark spirits here. Eventually it may manifest itself by pushing you down, scratching you, causing division in your relationship, or even making you sick." I kept going on as she listened intently, "You said it is following you around the house even into your bathroom which should be private. It probably also hangs out in your bedroom. So far, you are unaware of it. It may be capable of seductive gestures or sexual attacks upon you. There is no good fruit that it produces."

I told her it may be a conjured up familiar spirit or a dark spirit guide, or it could be something worse. I explained that many people dabble in witchcraft and the occult without understanding the spiritual doors they've opened to themselves and their family members. Darkness likes to hide. It may not reveal itself for years, unless the Lord's emanating light exposes and causes it to manifest in His presence.

(continues in the next chapter)

CHAPTER 27

TRUTH PREVAILS IN KAREN'S HOUSE - PERSISTENCE PAYS OFF

(PART 2 OF 2)

In this chapter:
- Recognizing the Deception of Darkness and the Authority You Carry
- Releasing Demonic Attachments From Objects and Commanding Them to Leave

Karen was shaking her head, "No" as I was speaking to her. She was convinced that it was Bubba's grandmother's spirit there to protect them, possibly as a spirit guide. I recognized that Karen wasn't going to budge on her deceptive beliefs. Then the Lord came to the rescue. He loves His children! The Lord planted a thought in my mind that made me smile. I already saw the results in my mind before I acted on it.

Recognizing the Deception of Darkness and Authority You Carry

I told Karen, "The Lord wants to show you the dark spirit that you think is Bubba's grandmother." She asked, "How is He going to do that?" I asked Karen, "Where in the house do you feel its presence the most?" She said, "When I do the dishes I feel her standing behind me." *It's amazing because there are a few other people I prayed for with almost the exact same scenario.* I then asked Karen to stand with her back against the sink and face me as I stood in front of her about five feet away. I said the Lord was going to release this bound spirit, presumably the grandmother, as I commanded it to stand right where I stood and face Karen. I then told her to close her eyes and look directly at me when I tell her to open her eyes. Karen wasn't afraid because she believed it was Bubba's grandmother spirit. She closed her eyes and then I spoke, "In the name of Jesus Christ of Nazareth I command the dark spirit in this house known by Karen to be Bubba's grandmother to come immediately and stand where I am standing and face Karen so she can see you!

And I break the power of any deception and command you to reveal to her who you really are. I rebuke any disobedience in Jesus' name."

Suddenly I felt its presence standing almost in my place. The hairs on my arms felt like they all were standing up. I informed Karen that it is standing in front of me facing her right now. I told Karen to open her eyes and look at me. Karen quickly opened her eyes and screamed as she quickly covered her face with both of her hands! She continually cried out, "Make it go away, oh my God! Make it go away!" I commanded it in Jesus' name to leave the room and I could feel it leave. Remember, Karen has knowingly given this dark spirit legal permission to stay in her house!

I quickly asked Karen, "What did you see?" She said it was tall and it was wearing a brown hooded robe. The hood was on its head but there wasn't a head or face in the hood that she could see. It was just black inside. It was holding a tall bent stick with a short handle near the middle, and the stick had a half-moon shaped piece of metal on the top end of it. She drew the description of the stick with her finger in the air as she described it to me. She mentioned again that she couldn't see a face in the hood.

Karen was a little shaken up and said she felt like she almost lost her breath when she saw it. I told her, "You don't want this dark reaper spirit of death living in your house." Wow, what an amazingly quick attitude change she had concerning allowing this reaper spirit and possibly other hidden cohorts to stay in her house. I told Karen that it would be easy to get rid of it, now that she was willing.

Karen wanted to call Bubba, her boyfriend, to tell him that it was not his grandmother's spirit living in the house and that instead it was the reaper's spirit of death voice that spoke her name. I encouraged her not to call him yet because it's connected to him in the spirit. Again, I told Karen, "You don't want this dark spirit in your house! And if you call Bubba now, he won't believe you and he will not want you to make his grandmother's spirit leave. In fact, spiritually, it is probably already speaking to Bubba. I guarantee you he will be calling shortly acting upset and will want to know who is here."

Karen said, "Bubba never calls home from his work." I assured Karen, "He will call shortly. I already sense it." I confirmed that Karen was the sole owner of her house, so she had the full authority and right to command this dark spirit to leave. At that point Karen wasn't sure if she was truly saved and became very concerned about it. So she willingly repeated the Salvation Prayer 1 and 2 (See Appendix).

Releasing Demonic Attachments From Objects and Commanding Them to Leave

Karen didn't want to put Bubba's grandmother's art piece outside, because he told her it was priceless to him. I had anointing oil with me, so with Karen's permission, I Anointed and blessed the metal art piece and verbally broke the power of any connotation or curse of darkness that was placed on it including all cohorts. I pleaded the cleansing Blood of Jesus over it completely and dedicated it to Jesus Christ of Nazareth. We commanded the darkness to leave her house and never return, in Jesus' name. Karen stood next to me and spoke also agreeing with everything I said. She decided to place Bubba's grandmother's metal artwork piece in the garage, then eventually out of her house.

I told her that her boyfriend would call within five minutes. Although Karen didn't agree with me, I told her again, He will call you and be adamant believing that somebody is here. That's because the enemy is angry and wants him to come home immediately since you cast It off his Grandmothers piece of art and out of your house. That dark spirit is telling him that you are cheating on him with somebody who is here. His suspicion will be on overdrive." Right after explaining to Karen the enemy's plan, her phone rang. Karen looked at me surprised and said, "It's Bubba. I can't believe it. He never calls from work. She answered the phone, and her first response was, "Nothing is going on! With an astonished puzzled look on her face, she continued to say, "Nothing is going on here." Karen walked into another room to continue her conversation. After a minute or so she came out of the room stating Bubba angrily grilled her then hung up on her.

I asked Karen how long it would take for Bubba to drive home. She told us about 40 minutes, but she assured us that he works until 4:30 in the afternoon. But I told Karen, "He doesn't believe whatever you told him, and I sense he will be rushing home. The dark reaper spirit you just kicked out of your house hates you for what you did to it. Now Bubba is being deceived and he's experiencing the dark spirit's anger. He's experiencing the spirit's betrayal feelings, believing these suspicious feelings are his own."

I asked Karen, "If you had a choice, would you allow Bubba to keep his 'believed' grandmother's spirit in your house?" Karen said, "Definitely not, no way, I saw that thing." I informed Karen that Bubba may choose that spirit of deception over her! "I sense a lot of arguments between you and Bubba if he continues living in your house. In fact, I believe he will leave within a week."

"If that's the case, it will be his loss. He can go live with that reaper spirit somewhere else," Karen said. Fifteen minutes had passed since Bubba's phone call and we were walking out of her house to go home. Surprisingly, Karen was right behind us. She didn't want to be there either if Bubba came home early with that accusatory attitude he had on the phone. She decided to go visit a friend for a few hours and see how it would all play out.

I heard from Karen's mother about two weeks later. She told me that Karen and Bubba had some intense arguments and he moved out four days after our visit. Karen had not felt the dark spirit presence since we prayed.

The Lord works in mysterious ways to rescue His children from evil! The Lord exposes deceptive hidden agendas and He reveals the truth. He allows us to make our own choices regarding who we want to follow or trust. We reap what we sow in our lives.

It is amazing how many people unknowingly have demonic entities attached to their personal property with different degrees of revealing manifestations. This can include land, water, houses, records, spiritual game boards, pictures, jewelry, or antiques. Most of these dark entities like to stay in the dark or hidden and may not manifest unless they feel threatened or exposed to the presence of the Lord's light. Usually darkness that is attached to objects in a house will manifest it's presence by secretly tormenting the family members in various ways.

CHAPTER 28

THE GIRL WHO DIDN'T KNOW HER HEIRLOOM JEWELRY WAS CURSED

(PART 1 OF 2)

In this chapter:
- A Divine Appointment to Better Understand the Enemies Tactics
- The Hidden Work of Darkness Manifesting
- The Lord Exposes Hidden Darkness Attached to Jewelry

A Divine Appointment to Better Understand the Enemies Tactics

Do you know someone with a persistent negative or demonic oppression in their life? When you try to identify the source of this oppression, it's important to ask the person if they received or inherited any jewelry or other items. It's surprising how often jewelry carries a family curse, familiar-spirit, spirit-guide, or other demonic attachments. Unfortunately, the recipient of the heirloom is seldom aware of past incantations prayed over it and how this may be affecting their life. They'll typically say that they're unlucky or a dark cloud follows them around.

The Lord had me in the right place at the right time to teach me about this very topic. And again, I have to say the Lord's love for His children is amazing!

I write these true-life experiences to reveal truths and to encourage you to allow the Lord to use you to set the captives free and lead them to Jesus Christ as their Lord and Savior. This will definitely put a smile on Jesus' face and yours. You will feel the joy and blessing of being His vessel of love as He changes people's lives right before your eyes.

I'd say it's more exciting being used and watching the Lord set many people free than winning the lottery (Although I never won one!) Eternal treasures are being stored in heaven for you as His heart moves your heart to act in obedience to His voice to help a person in need (Matthew 6:19-20). You'll help them in assistance, encouragement, prayer, Godly wisdom, in whatever is possible. And in Christ Jesus, well, we know all things are possible through Him (Philippians

4:13). It's also very important to know or understand that you can support prayer ministries financially if you are unable to participate physically setting the captives free. You can financially support a Church Ministry or missions to help those who are involved in changing people's lives through Christ Jesus. The spiritual rewards you begin to store in heaven are the same spiritual treasures as the ministry doing the physical outreach you support. Start storing a mountain of treasures in heaven — it's scriptural. Amen!

It's very important to Jesus to lead others to Him so they can receive His free gift of salvation, because He doesn't want one person to be absent from His Father's presence when their life on this earth comes to an end. Being absent of the body is being present with the Lord (2 Corinthians 5:6-8). As it is written nobody can come to the Father but by Me (Jesus Christ) (John 14:6).

A divine appointment the Lord used to teach me was when I went on a mission trip with my church for a week. It was a big tent camp meeting which involved a few churches. My pastor and his team were going to teach and minister the "Message of the Father's Love." The team from our church (including me) ministered after each message that our pastor taught and the Holy Spirit moved powerfully touching people's lives. A few hours after an evening service one of the visiting teenagers relinquished some occultic literature pieces and demonic paraphernalia. He was so touched and convicted by the Holy Spirit during the ministry time that he confronted one of the local pastors at the camp and said a friend gave it to him a few weeks earlier because he showed interest in it. He didn't know why he brought it with him to the church camp meeting.

So, on the same night the local pastor invited all the teenagers to the large tent where the meetings were held and gave a short teaching about the spiritual dangers and consequences of trafficking or being enticed with darkness. Following that teaching and prayer they made a fire in a burning barrel and allowed the teenager of his own free will to bring the demonic material forward. The teenager discarded all the demonic material into the fire. There were about 10 teenagers in attendance.

The Hidden Work of Darkness Manifesting

I stood there with two other team members just observing. As I looked around the big tent, I observed someone behind us about 30 feet away with her back toward us and her face almost touching the inside of the tent. This raised a red flag in my spirit, because sometimes the enemy causes a person to isolate themselves from the group. I have seen this many times before when darkness is afflicting someone or attached to them in some degree. It starts to manifest on a person causing them to turn their backs to the presence or the altar of the Lord (Acts 26:18). I quietly walked up behind her and heard her softly speaking to herself. She didn't know I was there.

She was forcibly rubbing the palms of her hands together back-and-forth saying, "I hate when this happens. I can't stop my hands from burning." I had the quick thought that perhaps she had dabbled or participated in some form of darkness in her past and that she (the darkness attached to her) was experiencing the burning fire on her hands as the demonic paraphernalia was being burned in the fire behind her. It was as if her hands had participated at some time in demonic activity. I was curious to see what was going to happen, so I stepped a little closer to her and said, "Do you need help with something?" She was surprised and jumped around and faced me.

I recognized her as one of the worship leaders from one of the other churches. She was a singer. She started to quietly growl at me when I asked, "Why do you feel your hands burning?" I quickly placed my hands on both sides of her face and rebuked it in Jesus' name. She started walking backwards while I was still holding her head and keeping her facing me as I spoke and commanded it to leave. Her growling quickly became intense as she continued rapidly walking backwards flipping chairs up and away from her as if they were weightless and as if she had eyes behind her head knowing where the chairs were situated. She tried to exit the tent walking backwards as I was still holding her head facing me. The darkness was still growling in bursts, but it appeared to be very fearful.

She was trying to exit the tent to get away from the anointing that was present inside the tent from consecutive ministry prayer meetings, and from the recent prayers that the teenagers were engaged in. The pastor and the teenagers had left just minutes before the girl started to manifest. I made a wide turn directing her toward the middle of the tent as she continued walking backwards trying to get away from me. I was thinking about her position in her church as the worship leader and asked myself, "Why didn't they recognize or discern this issue sooner?"

I will return to the story shortly, but there is something I need to repeat from earlier stories that is often forgotten.

This information will answer some questions you may have in this current story. The Lord is in control. You and I do not make the enemy manifest. The presence of the Lord in you makes the enemy manifest if the Lord chooses to allow it. If darkness manifests in your presence, realize that the Lord is showing you that He wants to set that person free. He wants to use you as His vessel to take part with Him in that person's deliverance. Remember, don't ever be afraid, because you are never alone. The Lord is always with you. He will teach you what to say and do, always keep your eyes and heart on Him, not on the manifesting darkness (the defeated enemy). Many people believe or think that they are under siege by the enemy. We have to lose this under siege mentality and realize that the enemy is the one under siege as we move forward holding up the light of Christ, being more than conquerors in Jesus. This understanding will benefit your ministry and eliminate any fear, that doesn't belong to you anyway!

Hollywood movies distort the truth by portraying dark forces as ominous and undefeatable. Many churches avoid the subject altogether. Unfortunately, some pastors instill fear in their congregation concerning deliverance and demonic manifestations. This spirit is passed on to others in the church because the pastors themselves have no experience or encounters with manifesting darkness. They've chosen not to get involved. The crafty enemy uses this fear and speaks into their ears they could lose many church members if they address the issues of demonic activity or manifestations.

Prayer ministers often ask the popular question, "Can a manifesting demon jump or transfer to them when they pray for someone who is manifesting?" So, I ask them, "Did they jump or transfer onto Jesus?" And the answer is, of course, "No!" They wanted no part of Him. They just wanted to get away from Him.

The same is true for you! Demons will not have permission to transfer as long as Jesus is your Lord and Savior and you're not willfully living a sinful life with any open doors in the spirit realm. You are created in His perfect image! Christ, the Anointed One, the Victorious Warrior lives in you. It is written that you will do even greater things because Christ resides in you. "Very truly I tell you, whoever believes in Me will do the works I have been doing, and they will do even greater things than these, because I am going to the Father. And I will do whatever you ask in my name, so that the Father may be glorified in the Son. You may ask Me for anything in My name, and I will do it" (John 14:12-14). The more practice the Lord gives you, the more comfortable, confident, and bold in Christ you will become. So start asking the Lord to send you divine ministry appointments. Ask the Holy Spirit to teach and use you to set His children free from apparent darkness that He reveals afflicting that person. Remember the battle is the Lords!

Very frequently, I've watched a demon or demonic entity quickly manifest before it was detected because of the presence of Jesus. Sometimes it's before the ministry, but usually it is during the ministry. It can pop up before it is addressed in prayer and it can temporarily, but not commonly, jump onto or climb on a person who is standing close by observing the ministry. The demon's intention is to get away from Jesus Christ's presence in you. His presence in us rattles their cage. Seldom a discerning observer may feel its creepy presence on them and may alert you if it's prolonged. *I'll explain this later.*

Sometimes fear or a spiritual open door may attract It to that person. The open door may have been created by some continual sin being committed in the person's life. I haven't experienced that issue often, because I command them to go directly to Jesus Christ of Nazareth, NOW, for Him to deal with as we minister. In all my years of ministry I have never experienced a demon jumping on me nor would I expect that to happen. If I ever experience that situation, I would instantly command it to get off me and go directly to Jesus Christ of Nazareth as I brush it off with my hand.

At times church observers or translators (when ministering in other countries) may begin to manifest as they translate what we are speaking to the person we are ministering to. There have been occasions when the translator started to tremble or their teeth shuddered slightly. Sometimes they were unable to speak (translate) out the prayers or the counsel we wanted translated, because they were emotionally touched or became teary eyed by the ministry they were translating to the other person. As a result, the Lord healed both of them and sets them free. This happened more often to us during private ministry when the person needing prayer brought a friend for moral support. The presence of the Lord's love ministered healing to both of them revealing Himself as if He orchestrated or planned a divine appointment. It's amazing and fun to observe and witness what the Lord will do! He reveals the tiniest forgotten (hidden) hurt and brings it out into His light. Healing comes, a profound release to the person's life.

We are betrothed to the Lord to become His Bride (John 3:29). He intensely loves those who receive Him. He has died for us, redeeming us from spiritual death. He is our protector, and He is in charge of the ministry He sets before us. Do not let fear or fear of the enemy and the unknown cripple you or your church when it comes to the ministry of setting the captives free. Actually, one should believe and walk in His victory always. He loves the saved and unsaved and wants them all to receive Him.

Now! If you have not received Jesus Christ in your life as Lord and Savior and decide to confront spiritual darkness in your own flesh and spirit (your own ability) and not by the Spirit of God, then that's another issue (Acts 19:11-20). Jesus is the only true deliverer and protector in the Spirit, setting the captives free (Luke 4:18).

Back to the story...

The Lord Exposes Hidden Darkness Attached to Jewelry

As we stood in the middle of the tent, I said, "I command the darkness, in Jesus' name, to release her and let her speak to me!" She stopped growling and I took my hands off her head. She stood there looking confused while two of her friends came to help her. Her two friends got a glimpse of her behavior and heard the growling before the enemy released her to talk to me. The darkness was still there, but it wasn't manifesting. Her friends were asking her questions and I realized she didn't remember anything of what just happened. She only remembered that I asked if she needed help. She was a single girl in her late 20s.

I asked her if she was ever involved in any occultic practices like Ouija boards or witchcraft. She asserted, "NO," and that she was saved and received the Lord when she was seven years old. I asked about her parents and siblings and I was informed that no issues of darkness existed. We commanded the darkness and all cohorts that manifested to stand at attention and not to move, in Jesus' name. As we prayed and broke the power of any curses, negative words spoken over her, familiar spirits, or unforgiveness, she started to manifest and growled at us again as we were asking her questions.

I asked the Lord to show us what right has she given for this bold and fearful demonic presence to stay. As I mentioned earlier, the enemy is legalistic. It was probably midnight by this time when a team member described a vision that morning of a gold heart with a gold circle around it. He said that it looked exactly like the pendulum on the necklace she was wearing. I thought to myself, "That's it! The darkness is attached to her jewelry." I asked her how she acquired the necklace and bracelet she was wearing and she said, "My mother gave it to me. It's been passed down in our family for generations." Without telling her why I asked if she could take off all her jewelry and give it to her girlfriend standing next to her to hold. Although I only noticed that she was wearing the necklace and a bracelet I asked if she was wearing any ankle bracelet or toe rings which are usually forgotten about. As her friend held the two pieces of jewelry we prayed for her again. This time there was no demonic manifestations or growling and she appeared alert and aware.

But within twenty seconds of praying her girlfriend who was holding her jewelry screamed. She dropped the jewelry on the ground proclaiming it burnt her hand and said it instantly got very hot as we were praying. I put more anointing oil on the palms of my hand and rubbed both of my hands together spreading the oil over both palms. I bent down and picked up the jewelry in my hand feeling no heat from it. I spoke out and blessed the jewelry anointing it while breaking the power of any darkness attached to it and dedicated the two pieces to the Lord. As I anointed the jewelry the girl who had been holding it was mumbling something I didn't understand. I thought she was praying in agreement over the jewelry with us, but when I looked at her, I noticed a fearful look on her face. She was staring at her arm and slowly raising it from her side. I asked her, "What's wrong?" With a frightened look on her face she exclaimed, "It's on my arm!" I said, "What's on your arm?" She said it was a big spider that came off the jewelry when I anointed and prayed over them. She was seeing the spider in the spirit, not in the natural. Although I didn't see it in the spirit, I quickly brushed my hand down her arm to get it off her and commanded it, in Jesus' name, to go directly to Jesus Christ of Nazareth for Him to deal with. Then I asked, "Is it gone?" She nodded her head, "Yes." She looked relieved but a little puzzled about what happened. She said, "It just disappeared after you prayed."

(continues in the next chapter)

NOTES

CHAPTER 29

THE SPIRITUAL SPIDER MANIFESTATIONS CONTINUED

(PART 2 OF 2)

In this chapter:
- Jesus' Love Reveals the Enemies Presence and Sets Us Free
- The Crystal Bracelet Explodes at the Mention of Jesus' Name

Jesus' Love Reveals the Enemies Presence and Sets Us Free

Then suddenly two boys who were standing next to her and observing as we prayed stood stiffly and appeared frightened. One was looking at the top of his leg and the other was holding out his arm staring at it fearfully. I asked if there was something on them and both responded, "Yes!" One of them, seeing in the spirit, said it was a spider. I felt a righteous anger rise up in me! Later, I realized it was the Lord's anger that I felt. I laid my hands-on top of his head and ran my hands simultaneously down both sides of his body — I was pushing everything and anything of darkness off his body. Then I quickly did the same to the other boy with my hands eventually hitting the dirt floor next to his feet. I looked up at them and asked if everything was off of them. They were excited saying, "Yes," but one pointed and said, "There are two spiders running away over there." The girl, the one I originally wiped the spider off her arm agreed and said she was seeing the two spiders running up the big tent pole. As she pointed at them one of the boys agreed and pointed with his finger following the spiders moving up the pole. Then they told me the spiders were sitting near the top of the tent pole which was about 25 feet high. The end of the pole was sticking through the top of the tent. Although I didn't see the spiders which were in the spirit, I pointed my finger up at them and commanded them not to move, in Jesus' name. Then I asked the Lord to have His warrior angels come and remove them. Within seconds, the woman and the boy both said the spiders were gone. I asked, "Where did you see them go?"

The boy told me that it looked like they were both sucked up through the small space between the tent pole and the tent where the pole protrudes through the roof of the tent. Being curious, I asked him, how did he know they were sucked out and didn't walk up and out. He said they didn't walk anywhere. The higher spider was facing down the pole and the lower spider was facing up. They were both close together when suddenly the top one appeared to be sucked up backwards through the small space or hole, but he said both were sucked out as one. "It almost looked like a cartoon," he said, "It happened so fast." He didn't see anything else after that."

I looked over at the girl we originally prayed for and saw that she put her jewelry back on. She was wearing her bracelet and necklace again which surprised me after she witnessed the ordeal that just took place. I walked over to her and asked if I could pray for her again. Without hesitation, she said, "Sure!" I wanted to make sure that the darkness was totally gone from her and the jewelry. I said a quick prayer and I blessed her and the jewelry again. Under my breath, I commanded any hidden or attached darkness to manifest itself, in Jesus' name. Nothing happened, and the girl just shrugged her shoulders and said, "I think everything is gone." Then I quickly prayed over the other girl who held the jewelry and I prayed over the two boys, too, declaring a hedge of protection over them. Finally, we all left the tent and went to bed.

I saw the girl the next morning still wearing her jewelry and I asked how things were going and she said, "Great!" I advised her to put all of the jewelry she owned into a bag when she got home and bring it to her pastor to be anointed and blessed breaking any curses or dark presence that may be attached to them.

Many times the forms or characteristics of a dark (demon) spirit may be totally different looking than what they portray. They can use visual deception to deceive us. They want to purposely hide their true identity attempting to protect the enemy's work, its purpose, or any legal invitation or permission that a person may have given them to stay. Depending on the situation and as the Lord leads me, I may directly speak to the demon or dark spirit and break the power of all deceptions, including visual deception, and command it to reveal itself as it truly is to the person being afflicted during ministry. This occurs more often when darkness is attached to reoccurring nightmares or is manifesting its many deceptions in a person dealing with relationships with dark spirits and multiple personalities. I will discuss those spiritual debilitating issues in another book that I'm writing concerning multiple personalities and recurring nightmares.

The Crystal Bracelet Explodes at the Mention of Jesus' Name

One day my wife, Rebecca and I participated in a local church fundraising event. We were selling a variety of landscape photographs taken while ministering in other countries. There were close to 75 exhibitors participating that day.

A woman from a nearby exhibit wanted one of our photographs for her husband, but was only interested in doing a trade. Her exhibit was full of brightly colored beaded and crystal bracelets. To help the woman, Rebecca agreed to the trade and picked out one of the crystal bracelets and wore it the rest of the day.

A few hours later, at the close of the exhibit, we packed our display and photos into two vehicles and began to drive home. I was following Rebecca in my truck. Within five minutes of driving, she called to tell me the bracelet suddenly exploded off her wrist! I asked her what happened?

Immediately after getting into the car, Rebecca felt that she needed to pray and bless the bracelet just-in-case any spiritual darkness was attached to it. We both knew from past experiences, crystals are often used in occultism. As Rebecca began to pray and bless the bracelet in Jesus' name, it exploded off her wrist before she could finish saying Jesus' name. The crystals flew everywhere in the car.

When we arrived home, it took a while to find all of the crystals that were scattered inside the car. They were on, under and in the cracks of the front and back seats. They were also on the front and back floors as well as in the rear window area. They were everywhere! I was shocked to see how scattered they were. We collected and discarded all of the bracelet pieces and eventually burned them in our garbage burning barrel.

We are grateful the Lord protects us from unseen spiritual darkness by removing it from our possession. It's important to bless and pray over jewelry regardless of where it comes from or how beautiful it looks.

NOTES

CHAPTER 30

PASTOR EDDIE

(PART 1 OF 3)

In this chapter:
- An Impartation of the Heavenly Father's Love
- Empowering the Church and Its Leaders
- Don't Waste Time Praying for Symptoms – Ask Questions and Find the Root Cause

An Impartation of the Heavenly Father's Love

I was on a team of thirteen people with my pastor for a two-week ministry trip to Africa. Part of our trip was preplanned and arranged in advance to include a one-day ministry conference for local pastors, "Ministering in the Power of the Heavenly Father's Love." We scheduled three sessions, morning, afternoon, and night, for thirty-five to forty pastors from the local area churches.

Each session was formed as a Biblical building block teaching and revealing how much their Heavenly Father loves them regardless of their sins. Although our Heavenly Father hates the sins we commit, He does not withhold His unconditional love from us, like many family members or friends may do, the normal world's response. The pastors were challenged to see themselves through their Heavenly Father's eyes and then encouraged to see their congregation and everyone else through His eyes. "Deep Calls To Deep" (Psalm 42:7).

Empowering the Church and Its Leaders

Most of the Pastors were getting set free or delivered during the prayer ministry at the end of each session. Many pastors were crying with emotion as their Heavenly Father revealed Himself to them in a tangible way. The Lord worked powerfully as they received revelation, conviction, and healing, freedom from many past and present hurts and issues. They released them all to the Lord. The joy of the Lord fell upon them that night during ministry with times of refreshing (Acts 3:19-21). They received a powerful touch of the Lord that day, a freedom that many never felt before and some never knew existed. Their lives will never be the same. We have to realize that all their churches will also reap blessings, because the pastors' lives had changed. They can impart this to their congregations. They can give away everything they received (John 7:37-39).

That night while most of the pastors were laughing in the joy of the Lord, I noticed one pastor standing with his face close to the wall with his arms and hands lifted and laughing as if the joy of the Lord was on him.

When a person isolates themselves from the group by turning their back away from the altar of the Lord or the congregation of any size while the Holy Spirit is moving powerfully, my spiritual discernment recognizes this as a possible red flag.

I approached the pastor from behind who was loudly laughing with his hands in the air giving the impression that he was worshiping the Lord. I placed my hands on his shoulders and quickly turned him around to face me. I recognized a demonic presence on him because his eyes were completely rolled back in his head resulting in totally white eyeballs. He continued laughing as if I never touched him. He was a tall man with a big face. I reached up putting my hands on both sides of his face and tilted it down towards me. Nothing changed, he didn't seem to acknowledge my presence. I looked at him and spoke, "In Jesus' name, I command all darkness to come into the light right now." Suddenly, he let out a long, distressing sound and fell to the floor. He appeared to be unconscious. I told a couple of team members to let me know when he stands up because the Lord wants to set him free from something. I didn't want him to leave without additional prayer. With all of the ministry going on around him I felt it wasn't time to address his dark spiritual issue. I continued to minister to others as the Lord led.

Don't Waste Time Praying for Symptoms – Ask Questions and Find the Root Cause

About an hour later as the ministry was coming to an end, I saw the tall pastor getting ready to leave. I walked up to him smiling while pointing at him saying, "Hey, the Lord wants to set you free from some dark hold the enemy has in your life." He responded in a low deep voice saying, "Yes, brother, sometimes we'll have to get together and meet so we can discuss it and maybe you can help me." I responded saying, "Discuss what?" Eddie said, "I have these 'things' happening to me at night for a few years and I don't know how to stop it." He told me that he had fasted and prayed but nothing ever changed. I told him that we were going to have the meeting right now and see what's going on and he respectfully agreed. I invited another team member to join us as we sat near the back of the room for more privacy.

I asked Eddie how was his relationship with the Lord? "I don't know. It could be better," he said. Then I asked him, "How do you think the Lord sees you and how do you see Him in your relationship?" He seemed a little agitated concerning this question. He asked me what does this have to do with his problem. I said it has everything to do with this problem and others you may be facing personally, spiritually, or with your congregation. I realized the enemy had blocked his ears from hearing a large portion of the teaching and ministry about the Father's love for His children during that full-day conference. I asked him how long he'd been a pastor and he said, "About 20 years." Pastor Eddie looked to be in his mid to late 40s with a pleasant composure and temperament.

I asked him more questions. "What is going on in your life? What do you think the dark spiritual attachment is all about?" He said he married his wife fifteen years ago and she belonged to a different tribe. Both tribes, so both families, disagreed with or rejected the marriage. Inter-tribal marriage was not acceptable or tolerated at that time with tribal elders. It took many years for the families to accept that they were married.

Eddie went on to tell me that he was a police officer for a few years before he became a pastor. He said he learned to walk in authority and judge fairly to resolve problems in the communities he served. He said police officers were not liked or trusted in most communities because of rampant corruption. The corruption caused innocent people to choose between forced payoffs or being arrested on a bogus charge. The police took advantage of innocent people who had money to pay them. Eddie was proud that he never took advantage of people in any way.

Eddie believed that the spiritual darkness came as a curse upon him because he married out of his tribe. I asked, "What is happening concerning this curse? How is it tormenting you?" He leaned towards me and slowly said, "I have these women who come to me in the night and they do these things to me." I said, "What things?" At first, he looked down at the floor and didn't respond. Then he slowly raised his eyes and looked at me. So, I said, "Do you mean they do sexual things to you?" Eddie responded in a quiet whisper with a long resounding, "Yeeeees." I asked him if these women were real or spiritual. He said, "They walk into my bedroom at night and they are real women." I was a little confused about his description, so I asked him if he was still married? He said, "Yes I am and my wife lives with me in our house." I asked if his wife knew about these visits and he responded with a drawn out "No." I asked if his wife slept in a different bedroom or do they sleep together in the same room? He said that they always sleep together in the same bed. His answer from the last question confirmed what I originally thought, but some of his answers were indicating otherwise. I told Eddie, "You are referring to spiritual beings that look like woman, but they appear to you in a physical form!" Eddie was quick to disagree saying, "No, they are real physical women."

I smiled as I watched the confused expressions of my team member's face. As I asked Eddie questions my team member's head went back-and-forth between Eddie and me as he watched and listened to each question and answer.

I had ministered to this issue before on two different occasions concerning men and enticing, spiritual, sexual encounters. Only one of the two men saw the spiritual being appear to be a beautiful woman. When he refused her sexual enticements she turned around and walked away. He said her back appeared to be on fire which he was unable to see as she approached him. Those two men did not understand the doors in the spirit they may have opened. They experienced a quick lesson about being naive. I also ministered to many women concerning this issue, but I will discuss that later. I will continue Pastor Eddie's spiritual sexual dilemma in the next chapter.

(continues in the next chapter)

CHAPTER 31

FREEDOM FROM DEMONIC SEXUAL STRONGHOLDS AND ENTRAPMENT

(PART 2 OF 3)

In this chapter:
- The Lord Reveals Truth So His Ministry Is Quick and Effective
- Forgiveness Is the Key to Freedom From Spiritual Darkness

The Lord Reveals Truth So His Ministry Is Quick and Effective

I told Eddie that the spiritual women he allowed to have sex with him for almost three years were actually demons. They were black and scaly with double-sets of teeth. By changing their spiritual appearance they deceived him into thinking they were beautiful women. Eddie said, "That can't be true." I told him I didn't care if he believed me or not, but it was most certainly true. I explained that he didn't know what truth was at this point! Usually, Succubus spirits sexually seduce men in their sleep. Eddie was beyond that point.

My next thought was to prove to him that these spirits were demons as I described. I thought about calling them fourth to stand in front of him allowing him to confirm their identities as the women that visit him. Then before his eyes I'd break their power of deception by commanding them to reveal their true identities and appearance, in Jesus' name. I knew that if Eddie really saw who he was participating with in these sexual encounters he would be repulsed and want to jump out of his skin. I was 99% sure this was a good idea, because if he could see them for what they really are, it would produce powerful good results that would permanently change his life concerning this issue. He would definitely sin no more in this arena.

BUT right then, the Lord's voice spoke to me concerning the remaining 1% and said, "Don't do that." I heard this strong in my thoughts. So I sat there with no direction. I asked the Lord in my thoughts, "What do you want me to do next?" The Lord hears our thoughts (Psalm 139). The Lord gave me a paragraph to speak to Eddie. So, I spoke every thought assertively and bluntly. I said "Your wife's tribe may have prayed against you and your marriage, but these demonic spirits started visiting you almost three years ago as you said. You were attracted to them because lust entered your heart. I don't know if you were faithful to your wife. You did lustful things with yourself getting the attention of a sexual, lustful and seductive dark spirit. This sexually seductive demon came to you sometime when you were alone and then again boldly when you laid next to your wife. You allowed this deceptive demon, posing as a beautiful woman, to do sexual acts to you that opened a second door to deeper demonic sexual intimacy. In a short time this dark spirit was visiting you almost every night enslaving you to its purposes. Then eventually, after a period of time as you loved what it did for you, a second seductive demon was invited (perceived to you as an additional beautiful woman). It came with the first one to perform their sexual acts together on you. You enjoyed the satisfaction of your hidden secret sexual escapades that your wife would never know of nor perform for you."

I said, "Possibly you chose to spend time with them over your wife." I told him, "eventually the two sexual demons became rough and the sexual acts started to hurt and you couldn't control the situation anymore. As you tried to stop It, they really caused you pain. They made a sex slave out of you and now you don't know what to do. You probably were afraid to go to sleep at night, because you found it very hard to wake up from your nightmare trans-like sleep once they came to you." I told Eddie that he could always call on the Lord in his thoughts and the Lord would hear him and move on his behalf. I also told him "But they made you feel unworthy to call out to Him for help and silenced your voice from yelling out for help when they were in your sleep captivated presence. They have imprisoned you in your sleep while they have their way with you."

As I was still speaking to Eddie the Lord dropped the next paragraph in my thoughts. I told Eddie that the tribe issue had been his mental excuse for the situation and that he had been lying to himself concerning that. I said, "The reason the dark sexual spirit came is because you invited It. You could have rebuked its presence around you when It first started, but you didn't. "It" continued to come more often, because you love what it does to you. Eventually the sexual demon invited Its friend and you received both of them."

I told Eddie that he committed adultery against his wife and also the Lord, because he will be part of the bride that the Lord is returning for. "You have done detestable things against the Lord by having sex with demons and the Lord hates it." The Lord is a jealous God concerning His bride (2 Corinthians 11:2). I agreed with Eddie that it was obvious that he didn't know how to get free on his own. "You may be unwilling to ask a brother pastor for help because you're afraid he would gossip the information concerning your secret sin, and how you were ensnared, which would spread like wildfire throughout the church community. Being exposed like that would cause you to be (temporarily) removed as a church pastor and to receive counseling and healing which the enemy would love. Possibly that was the enemy's plan from the beginning." The enemy "comes only to steal and kill and destroy." See John 10:10. That is Its fruit. Eddie humbly agreed with everything I spoke to him. I told Eddie that the Lord had heard his prayers. He loved him very much but hated his sins. I told him "He does not condone your sins which smells very unpleasant to Him (Ezekiel 20:41). But the Lord says He is a forgiving God and His great mercy abounds." (Joel 2:13). Eddie probably knew this already, but the Lord wanted to tell him again.

Then I told Eddie that the Lord was going to set him free because He showed me what He wanted him to do. "I think this is a divine appointment that He set up for you because He's heard your prayers for help," I said. I informed Eddie that getting set free is actually the easy part. But I said, "To stay free especially the first three weeks in this situation is the hardest part. Then it gets easier as you continue to abide in the Lord. The enemy will be totally angry when the Lord removes you from its grip. The enemy will try to barrage you with intense sexual temptations that you have never experienced before. They will want you back and can't stand watching you be free of them. The Lord will help you, but it's your choice not to allow yourself to sin, opening another spiritual door during the enemy's intense temptations."

I told him it is written, "Resist the enemy and he shall flee." Eddie asked, "How is the Lord going to set me free? Do I have to stand up or do anything?" I told Eddie to sit there for a minute, "I'll have you read a few scriptures as the Lord leads. This way you'll know His Words are speaking to you. Then we'll go from there."

Forgiveness Is The Key to Spiritual Freedom From Darkness

We went over the Bible verses and even though Eddie was a pastor, I asked him to repeat-after-me the Salvation Prayer: Parts 1 and 2 (See Appendix). We then covered the following seven points:

1. Eddie prayed and asked the Lord to forgive him for having sex with demons. He broke the power and renounced all spiritual demonic sexual soul-ties.

2. We also prayed asking the Lord to forgive him for committing adultery against his wife, and himself.

3. I directed Eddie to release any hatred or unforgiveness concerning his wife's family and tribe, and his family tribe. We broke the power of all curses against them and their children.

4. We broke the power of all negative words, vows, and curses that he may have spoken against himself or others. He renounced all the darkness and its power that he invited into his life

5. We spent some time with Eddie forgiving himself and renouncing his sin and then declaring the Blood of Jesus over himself, his church, and his family.

6. After this I had him bless himself, his family, and his church. We blessed all the plans the Lord had over his life.

7. Finally, we dedicated everything to the Lord pleading a hedge of protection around everything that affected their lives.

When we finished the prayers, Eddie looked at me and said, "Nothing happened! I didn't get set free!" I just smiled and said, "No, that's coming in a minute." I knew his release was going to manifest big time because the enemy had a deep root in his groin area that the Lord was going to remove. Many ministers believe that a person should or may vomit up a demon. Of course, I don't allow that enemy game playing to happen anymore. I don't allow it in the spirit and I don't allow it to manifest in the flesh. I commanded them to quietly get out now without getting pulled into any distractive demonic game playing.

Eddie was sitting on a movable 8-foot church bench and we sat on another one facing him. Just in case he followed the emotional tradition and threw up, I didn't want to be sitting in front of him. So we arranged ourselves without him realizing why. I sat about three feet to the right of him and the other team member sat three feet away to the left of him on the same bench facing his bench and his direction. As soon as we were situated I looked at Eddie and asked, "So are you ready to get set free?" Eddie just smiled and nodded his head yes. The Lord showed me earlier that he was going to be released when I grabbed his big belly, so timing wasn't a concern. I asked Eddie to put his hands on his seat next to him so his arms wouldn't block my access to his belly. Eddie had no idea what we were going to do. I had Eddie look over at me and I kept constant eye contact with him. I said, "In the name of Jesus Christ of Nazareth, I command all sexual spirits and their cohorts that afflict Eddie in any way to hear what I speak right now and I rebuke any disobedience. You have been renounced and we all come into agreement in what Eddie spoke and decreed (Matthew 18:19). Jesus Christ of Nazareth is Eddie's only Lord and Master. Eddie has repented and is forgiven from all of his sins. You have no more authority or access to him or over him (Psalm 103:12)." As I reached over with my left hand and grabbed his belly, I said "And right now," "I Release Eddie from all darkness! In Jesus name."

As soon as I said "Release" Eddie shook radically and let out a repeated loud roar as if he were having a convulsive fit during each long roar. He did not throw up at all, so I slid down the bench closer to him never letting go of his belly. I continued to speak out during his ordeal which lasted very intensely for a couple of minutes.

I commanded all of the dark residue and attachments including all of its cohorts to leave him and that nothing be left behind. I asked the Lord to flood all the continual emptying dark areas within him with the Abba Father's love. I asked the Holy Spirit to quickly crowd out all of the darkness that may try to hide. We were watching it happen very fast — out with the old (dark stuff) and in with the new (love of God and Light of His presence).

Eddie was wet with sweat when it was all over, but he was smiling from ear to ear. His face changed and he looked like a very happy young boy. He stood up and hugged both of us and he couldn't stop saying, "Thank you!" I said, "Thank the Lord. He is the one who set you free!" He held both of his hands straight up in the air and thanked Jesus for setting him free. He said he felt stuff leave him as we prayed and he said one thing was a little painful that left the groin area of his body. I explained that it was a root of the enemy that the Lord pulled out. Eddie kept shaking his head in amazement while again shaking our hands. He was obviously extremely happy and grateful. The whole ordeal took less than an hour, after we sat down.

The continuing important results of Pastor Eddie being released is explained in the next chapter!!!

(continues in the next chapter)

NOTES

_____

_____

_____

_____

_____

_____

_____

_____

_____

_____

_____

_____

_____

_____

CHAPTER 32

A STRATEGY TO MAINTAIN FREEDOM FROM DEMONIC SEXUAL TEMPTATIONS

(PART 3 OF 3)

In this chapter:
- Understanding Soul-Ties
- Your Spiritual Authority and Power to Resist Temptations
- Asking For and Receiving Forgiveness Equals Holy Spirit Power

Understanding Soul-Ties

I told Eddie that I wanted to talk to his wife to see if she was also being tormented by these sexual spirits. Usually in marriage or the consummation of two people, the two become one flesh supernaturally (Mark 10:8). That means by having sex together, soul-ties develop. Many times either spouse may have other sexual soul ties from past relationships, not realizing the possible spiritual consequences. Not always, but sometimes a dark spirit that attached itself to one mate years earlier (knowingly or unknowingly) may have access to affect or afflict the new mate or spouse. I run into this issue with women more than men. I believe women are more sensitive to a spiritual presence mainly when they sense something doesn't feel right, but they are unable to put their finger on the real issue. Men may discern that something doesn't feel right, but then without much thought shrug their shoulders and move on until the issue becomes extreme. Then they may seek help.

I told Eddie I would say nothing to his wife about tonight's ministry concerning him nor the issues he was dealing with. I asked him to bring his wife to the open church meeting the next day and I'd pray for her in general and see what happens. Eddie agreed to bring his wife the next afternoon. I reminded him again about the strong sexual temptations the enemy would exert on him attempting to get back what It lost.

I wanted to teach Eddie something quick before he left the church that night, so I asked him to stay a few minutes longer. I told him it would help alleviate most of the enemy's barrage of attacks toward him and its intense sexual temptations at night. Eddie sat down to listen

Your Spiritual Authority and Power To Resist Temptations

I told him I learned this spiritual warfare strategy from the Lord in earlier ministry experiences and it works. I've never heard anyone teach about it in the church (at large) before. It's very simple and has profound results if you believe in your authority through Christ Jesus. Ask the Holy Spirit to put a 'CHECK' in your spirit that alerts you, even if you are in a deep sleep. Ask the Holy Spirit to wake you up and warn you (sense) that the enemy is putting on it's boots and is getting ready to walk over the (spiritual) hill to you. (This "check" also works really well when dealing with anxiety or fear.) If the enemy gets close to you, it will torment, badger, make you fearful and entice you to sin. It's important to NOT WAIT until it's in your presence (where the battle is more intense) before you pray and start to rebuke it.

I went on to explain, "Learn to recognize the Holy Spirit's prompting alerting him of the enemy's coming before it leaves its camp. Start rebuking it immediately with your authority in Christ and command it to stay where it is and not to come over the hill to you with its evil seductive temptation's intentions in Jesus name. Immediately, or in a short time you will experience a lessening sense of its coming and peace will fill your concerns. You will be totally surprised by the excellent results as you speak your prayer commands out in advance before the attack of anxiety, temptations or fear arrive. Do not pray from inside your mind. You can speak commands in a whisper, if spoken in assertive authority in Jesus name. It's important that you OWN this prayer understanding in your heart. You have to believe in advance, because Jesus' authority in and through you makes it happen. Remember to ask Jesus that the enemy hears His commanding voice through you when you speak commands in His name. You will experience the positive results of less temptations if any at all. As you speak it WILL happen. Practice makes perfect." I told Eddie to "resist the enemy and he will flee from you." Its temptations may return at a later time but don't give It any place in your life! Speaking this prayer and understanding its power will increase your faith in your authority bringing victory and change to a person's life. "Eddie will experience its effectiveness," I assured him.

Eddie brought his wife to the open church meeting the next day and I introduced myself to her. I said, "I prayed over Eddie last night and I would like to pray a blessing prayer over you also." I wanted to see what the Lord was going to reveal. Eddie's wife Gloria mentioned that Eddie had been very excited and happy all last night and today about the torment and burdens the Lord freed him from. "He has been dancing around all morning like a big child!" She said that Eddie told her everything last night, but she never experienced these problems. I wasn't sure what Eddie had told her, so I asked, "What did Eddie tell you concerning the ministry he received last night?" Gloria said, "He told me about the two sexual women spirits that took advantage of him many nights for years." She said she was unaware of it all. But now Gloria knew most of the details and informed me that Eddie asked her for forgiveness for his grave sin and actions. He told her that he didn't know how to stop it. She said, "I forgave him, but I was a little upset that he never told me about it."

I was very surprised that Eddie told her practically everything. I remember feeling very proud of him in those moments because of his honesty and finally exposing the truth to his wife. I had noticed he was a little choked up. His heart was convicted last night as I had him ask the Lord for forgiveness for committing adultery against his wife and the Lord. He was unaware that he was committing adultery among other things during his actions.

I prayed for Gloria and she appeared to be fine. Maybe she had little or no physical relations with Eddie in the last three years or her spiritual light was much brighter than his. The enemy didn't want to get near her. Either way, it was good to see no dark manifestations as she was receiving prayer.

Early that night as the meeting ended my pastor paired up groups consisting of two or three members of our team who could go with some of the local pastors to minister in their churches for the next two days, Saturday and Sunday. Five teams or groups went out. The remaining team members stayed back to assist our pastor at the original host church. Each group would have two or three meetings on Saturday in two or three different churches and two meetings on Sunday. Late Sunday afternoon the groups would return back to the host church.

As my pastor was setting up the teams with the local pastors, he called me over and said, "I want to pair you up with Pastor Eddie. He's the lead pastor in charge of the Association of Pastors in this large region. He covers the leadership of all the pastors and their churches and heads up those who attended the pastor's conference." Then my pastor asked, "Have you guys met each other?" Eddie and I looked at each other and smiled. We both responded, "Yes, we have met each other." I was thinking to myself that I was glad I didn't know Eddie's leadership position at the time I was ministering to him. I may not have been so bold and direct with him, but the Lord knew that. Knowing this certainly gave me a better understanding of Eddie's fear concerns about trusting another pastor (which unfortunately is a problem there) gossiping about his demonic sexual entrapment and possibly intentionally exposing him to everybody. It also revealed the condition of the church there. The Heavenly Father revealed His unending passionate love, presence and truth to the pastors at the conference releasing and setting His shepherd's free.

It was great to hear the pastor's overall excitement about going back to their churches and becoming better pastors for their congregations and communities.

Asking For and Receiving Forgiveness Equals Holy Spirit Power

Pastor Eddie came late Saturday morning to pick up our team of three. He wanted to bring us to a late afternoon meeting at one of his churches. On our way it started to rain heavily which made the dirt roads very muddy. It was supposed to be a twenty minute drive, but the hilly road conditions slowed us down and cars in front of us were getting stuck. It took two hours to get there! His congregation was still worshiping the Lord when we arrived. The old church building walls around the structure were collapsed and the roof was supported by 4 to 6-inch diameter tree trunks.

After Pastor Eddie introduced us, he told the congregation that he was stuck in bondage for over two years and the Lord sent a team of people from America and used them to set him free. He started to again praise the Lord and his church joined him in prayer and praise thanking the Lord for his deliverance. Eddie didn't tell them what he was set free from, but the congregation of about sixty people didn't seem to care as they worshiped the Lord together. Our team spoke of the Father's love and then ministered to them. The Holy Spirit touched them powerfully.

On Sunday we ministered in two different churches that he also pastored. He introduced us and spoke about his recent deliverance to both of the congregations. They all clapped and gave praise to the Lord for at least three minutes thanking Him. He also apologized because his bondage may have held back the move of the Holy Spirit in the church.

The morning session was a combination of two churches which consisted of approximately 100 people, twenty of whom were children. After we spoke a second message of the Father's love to them, we asked the Holy Spirit to come and minister to their hearts. As they started to praise the Lord I noticed that all the children were either standing or kneeling in the front. Some were as young as five years old holding their hands in the air and praying out to the Lord with tears rolling down their faces. The presence of the Lord was on them as some started to cry praying out loud in their own language (I believed). I felt someone hold my arm and as I turned I noticed Pastor Eddie standing next to me crying and speaking to me. I couldn't understand him because the congregation's prayers and praises were loud. He pointed at the children and spoke in my ear saying that they were all praying in tongues, their spiritual languages.

He said that they had never praised the Lord like that before and that they were worshiping/praying in tongues which they never did before, Powerful! Pastor Eddie said, "They were never taught how to do that!" Still crying as he watched them, he lifted his hands in the air and gave thanks and praise to the Lord. The Holy Spirit moved among his congregation powerfully revealing the Father's heart to them. We stood and watched for about fifteen minutes and then we ministered personally with hands on the people who were still standing.

The second church that we ministered to later that day was fifteen minutes from the first one. About forty members were all worshiping the Lord when we arrived. It was almost a duplicate service as the earlier one. Pastor Eddie repeated the same introduction as members gave praise thanking the Lord. I can see Eddie was again deeply touched as the Heavenly Father's love consumed his church members powerfully!

It's amazing to watch the Lord's presence convict, heal, and release people. He was changing their lives right before our eyes. And it was also exciting to hear the other teams' experiences and testimonies when we returned to the host church on Sunday night.

NOTES

CHAPTER 33

A BRIEF UNDERSTANDING OF DEMONIC SEXUAL SPIRITS

In this chapter:
- Spiritual Sexual Encounters Becoming More Prevalent in Society
- Ministry in This Area Has Increased Significantly
- When Spiritual Sexual Nightmares Become Too Real to Deny

Spiritual Sexual Encounters Becoming More Prevalent in Society

Let me explain why demonic sexual spirits are invited intentionally or unintentionally manifesting Its sexual acts upon a person usually in their sleep. Internet, social media, TV, radio and sexual magazines are media platforms that contribute immensely to this growing problem. Sexual content is more publicly prevalent today than ever before. Much of our population is being desensitized even in their early years concerning sexual behavior and gratification.

Our younger generations try to communicate with spirits as they see them demonstrated on TV, not knowing that dark spirits may respond. They are unaware of the spiritual doors they open by lusting for sexual satisfaction. People also unknowingly open doors to spiritual and physical affliction by dabbling in witchcraft and spells, tarot cards, séances, Ouija boards, curses, sexual sin, masturbation, blood sacrifices, or watching evil and fearful movies. The spirit of fear manifesting on someone opens a door to many demonic spirits to afflict them. Some ignorantly invite dark or evil spirits to come into them, challenging and daring It to manifest. (I saw this on a TV show.)

Some people believe they are strong and can handle their secret sexual encounters with dark spirits whether seen or unseen in the spirit. When they realize the situation is getting intense and overwhelming and they are losing or have lost their imagined dominating control, fear consumes them. Reluctantly they willfully participated and opened a spiritual door and may possibly in time become a sex slave to the dark spirits. They don't know how to stop or get released from the tormenting and abusing grip of the enemy. It continues to steal, kill and destroy their lives in many ways. The tormented person fears going to sleep at night because of the sexual attacks. Sometimes the person will go into deep depression or sickness and begin taking prescription drugs or alcohol to find peace and contentment. Unfortunately, some are deceived by the constant voices of the enemy speaking in their thoughts to commit suicide to achieve their needed peace and freedom.

Many people do not know that Jesus Christ of Nazareth is the only person that has the authority to set them free, spiritually and physically, from all evil and demonic entrapment. Ignorance of sin committed may open spiritual doors and allow darkness to enter (1 Peter 5:8).

Sometimes the attachment of spiritual darkness is not noticed. It may not manifest for five or ten years leaving the victim clueless of the reason for the demonic access or the attacks. The only way to become free and shut those demonic spiritual doors is to ask Jesus Christ into your life to be your Lord and Savior. Then speak out and ask Jesus to forgive you of all your sins. In this case ask Him to forgive you for the sexual dabbling and enticements that lured you into addictions. Prolonged participation in this area can draw a person deeper into a demonic sexual relationship with demons that makes the person a captive of spiritual darkness and its games.

Ministry in This Area Has Increased Significantly

After asking for forgiveness, renouncing those sins and the enemy's work in your life, in Jesus' name. Ask the Lord to fill all those released dark areas in you with the Holy Spirit and the Father's love. Expect the inflowing of His Love to crowd out or push out everything that does not belong in you or on you leaving no residue, no darkness behind. This sounds simple, but it is profound and effective. The Lord does all the work. You just have to speak it out in His name and believe, releasing everything to Him.

I would definitely have another (saved) person present with you to agree in prayer. Through Jesus one person in prayer has the authority and power to cast out 1,000, but two people in agreement in prayer have the authority and power to cast out 10,000 (Deuteronomy 32:30). That is why Jesus sent out His disciples pairing them together by two's.

Many churches do not speak to their congregations about these growing ministry secret issues and they are more prevalent in the church today than ever before. The Army of God must learn and discern. We should recognize these issues and understand sexual spirits so we can be more effective in setting the captives free.

Just look at the issues of the incubus spirit. It's a sexual dark spirit that seduces women. The succubus spirit is a sexual dark spirit that seduces men. Once you receive their sexual enticements you may become captive to their sexually controlling endeavors. Eventually, they become rough and hurtful as they sexually abuse or rape you in your sleep. Usually the person feels paralyzed during this process and is unable to speak out as these demonic spirits have their way with you. In time these dark spirits invite other dark spirits like fear, condemnation, self-hatred, guilt. They may develop a spiritual stronghold in you as they attempt to draw you away from God and His plan for your life. They also attempt to rob the fruits of His Spirit in your life and replace them with the fruits of darkness. Most people believe they are experiencing a bad dream or a nightmare even though their body feels and responds to the sexual arousal sensations of their penetration. Some people sleep with their bedroom lights on and are afraid to go to sleep. Some resort to prescription meds or alcohol to lessen the feelings of their nightly uncontrollable experiences.

When Spiritual Sexual Nightmares Become Too Real to Deny

Many people never heard of this and don't understand why this is happening to them. Unfortunately others want to stay ignorant of these facts. They believe this truth of being spiritually sexually attacked as they sleep is impossible. It becomes their own tormenting secret because it sounds too insane to talk to anyone about. Many do understand and realize these attacks are real and not a nightmare, but they feel too embarrassed to talk about it or to expose it, and they don't know where to turn for help.

Secular counseling only assesses your issues and labels you with a negative diagnosis and prescribing medications. After months and months of prescription changes, an effective drug with little side effects may be achieved. But usually the drugs are not effective enough to completely deaden the nightly sexual attacks and physical sensations. The person may start to self-medicate by drinking alcohol or increasing their prescription intake or adding other over-the-counter drugs. This can lead to drug addictions, and possibly short or long-term side effects.

Most people do not want to expose this to leaders in their church, unfortunately. The enemy does not want to be expelled or identified, so it will induce intense fear in the person by speaking to their thoughts and convincing them of the embarrassment and rejection that will come, especially if it leaks out to church members. Sometimes the enemy uses a very powerful deception that even seasoned Christians have been deceived to believe.

The enemy sometimes convinces people that they have grieved the Holy Spirit and have committed the unpardonable sin and will not be forgiven by Jesus. The person believes they are condemned to hell and have forfeited the gift of salvation. The enemy is also successful with this convincing lie in many other areas of ministry. Truthfully, this is the situation the enemy is in. He is already condemned to hell by God and can't change Its future destiny (John 16:11).

But see, the Lord has mercy that abounds. He has mercy for anyone on earth who calls on His name and repents of their sins. No sin is too big for Him to forgive. Salvation is a breath away for anyone who asks Him for forgiveness. Do not let the enemy (father of lies) deceive you and rob you of the truth of your salvation that Jesus purchased for you on the cross. No one is an exception to receive the abundant and eternal life in and through Jesus.

CHAPTER 34

SPIRITUAL SEXUAL ENCOUNTERS - AWARENESS AND CAUSES OFTEN NOT SPOKEN ABOUT

In this chapter:
- Ministering to Someone Practicing Astral Projection
- Exposing the Spiritual Deception – "Jesus Is My Husband."

Ministering to Someone Practicing Astral Projection

Astral projection travel is usually an intentional out-of-body experience using meditation techniques or a trance-like state of mind allowing your spirit/soul to leave your body and travel throughout the spirit world. People who astral project can go through spiritual open doors perhaps to a place or even to a spiritual open door within another person. Now God translated people in the Bible to places He desired them to be for His purposes. Today there are many testimonies where the Lord translates a person. This is usually someone who has developed a relationship with Him, received Him as Lord, or whose heart intimately seeks Him. They are translated to places in the natural or in the spirit realm to fulfill His purposes. This translated process is under His authority and control.

However, astral projection travel is considered to be a counterfeit process to what God does that the enemy imitates. It allows a person to astral project themselves (spirit/soul) into the spirit world. This process is controlled and connected by dark forces including demons, spirit guides, or a light source that is not of God. The Lord sees it as idolatry, and it is detestable to Him because the source of its achievement is from darkness (Romans 8:9) (Leviticus 20:6). The Lord is a jealous God for us because He loves us and wants no other gods or idolatries that we could worship or commit to in place of Him (Exodus 34:14) (Deuteronomy 6:15). There are people who practice astral projection that have no evil intentions. They just want to escape reality for a while and travel out of their body in the spirit world and veg out. But the problem remains. Their source of movement and access in this process is not of God, but of darkness (Leviticus 19:31). People who astral project have to be careful of demons who also are present in the spirit world that may want to attach, hurt, abuse, or control them in travel. I've heard that when an aggressive demon confronts an astral projection traveler, that person may call on the name of Jesus Christ and the demon retreats or disappears. This has deceived some people who are actually projecting to believe that God (Jesus) approves of their activities because He, or the mention of His name, protected them (James 2:19).

Participants who believe they are not committing a sin before the Lord as they engage in astral projection are deceiving themselves. They are not believing what the heart of God reveals very clearly in Bible scriptures, but with itching ears look elsewhere (2 Timothy 4:2-4). When this person dies a natural death without repentance and believes they will live eternally in heaven, the Lord may say to them, "Depart from Me, I don't know you" (Matthews 7:21-23).

Those who are concerned about their eternal salvation and confused or uncertain about how the Lord Jesus sees their involvement in astral projection, should do the following:

The next time you astral project into the spirit world, call out in the spirit world and say, "Heavenly Father, in Jesus' name, I ask Jesus Christ of Nazareth and Him only to come speak to me now, because I want to ask a question." In seconds Jesus Christ of Nazareth will be in front of you. Make sure you test the spirit that comes to you by repeating to Him, "I want to speak to Jesus Christ of Nazareth and Him only" (1 John 4:1). There is a deceptive counterfeit dark spirit that answers to the name of Jesus and appears to have a light about him. Even though it only speaks lies of darkness, It has deceived many who are naive concerning the Word of God. So it is very important to ask for Jesus Christ of Nazareth. Then ask Him how He feels or thinks about your astral protection endeavors. You will be very surprised what He will speak to you as you are face to face with Him. You will believe and feel the truth of His words.

Now there are other people who astral project that have evil intentions in mind. They will travel through open doors in the spirit that people knowingly or unknowingly have opened within themselves. They may astral project alone or together with others or connect with demons. Individually or together they can torment, badger, or sexually attack (abuse) you among other things. Sometimes the person projecting has spiritual access through soul ties with people that they had intimate relationships in the past, in the natural world. This gives the astral projector an open door to access and torment sexually their former lovers and others unknown to them who have opened spiritual doors to themselves. A person using astral projection to sexually abuse others is not limited to nighttime (sleep) torment and sexual attacks.

It's important for anyone reading this to break the power of any soul ties or sins you have committed causing a spiritual opening in your life. Break that power in Jesus' name. Then proclaim the blood of Jesus over any spiritual open doors, in the name of Jesus Christ of Nazareth.

You must know and understand that people who astral project are not demons even though they may act or sound like one at times. Their body is still alive some-where as they astral project themselves out of their body. There is a silver cord attaching their spirit/soul to their bodies (Ecclesiates12:6-7). It is their lifeline that stretches out a very long distance into the spirit world enabling them to travel without getting lost there. It takes a lot of mental energy to persist in an astral projected state.

But concerning ministry they are not subject to obeying commands in Jesus' name, because they are not dead people and they are not demons. They may repeat back to you "in Jesus' name" any command you may have spoken to them as they manifest through a person you're ministering to. Although they can act and behave like demons this is one way to realize who you are dealing with. They can repeat that Jesus is fully God and fully man. Demons will not speak this. They can say, "the Blood of Jesus over me." Demons will not say, "the Blood of Jesus," rather they say, "the blood of pigs." Usually, astral projection spirit people will have a common name like Joe, Danny, Linda, or Mary, but demon names are usually weird sound-ing. If the Astral projecting person is tormenting someone that I am ministering to, I read 1 Corinthians chapter 13, the love chapter, to them once or twice. They can't handle hearing Scriptures about love. It usually drives them away. A couple of times I've convinced them to repent and repeat the sinner's prayer. Their attitudes actually changed after they received the Lord in their life and then they left the person they were tormenting. I often wonder if the person actually became saved through Christ Jesus in the natural.

When a demon is present with them, the demon may speak and then hide behind the astral projecting person as you rebuke it. I have much more to say about this issue. I'm including details in the multiple personalities and reoccurring night-mare book that I am writing. If you know you're dealing with a spirit who is astral projecting, I was informed of another remedy that works well. If you are saved, a child of God, this a good way to minister in this situation: First, warn them to leave the person, or you are going to cut and sever their silver cord with the Sword of the Spirit. Remember, "I can do all things in Christ Jesus, who strengthens me" (Philippians 4:13). Their silver cord is attached between their spirit/soul and their body. As their spirit/soul travels in the spirit world their bodies are "vegging out" somewhere in the natural world. If you cut their silver cord, their spirit/soul may become lost and unable to find its way back to reconnect to their bodies. This may leave their natural body separated existing in a veg state and eventually death wherever they are. The fear of you having this knowledge being able to sever their silver cord will cause them to leave your presence and the person they are tormenting. You should also tell them not to return, because this is their first and last warning. The people I have ministered to concerning negative astral projection encounters have received understanding and victory in this area of their life.

Exposing the Spiritual Deception – "Jesus Is My Husband."

I was approached twice for counsel in two separate instances five years apart at a distance of 800 miles between locations. This tells me that this ungodly, demonic, sexual deception belief experience may be more prevalent on a larger scale. The following secret sexual deception story will be informative and revealing to those who were deceived and victimized and to others hearing this for the first time. In both cases they were women in their sixties, one I met in the past approached me privately and wanted my feedback on something they seemed concerned about. In both instances they wanted me to promise that I wouldn't mention their name to anyone concerning our conversation. Both of their stories were very similar, so I will only give short details about one of them. They both attended a bi-weekly woman's prayer meeting for approximately three to four months. Each group consisted of three to six women. One of the women leaders from the group approached them asking a lot of questions about their intimate relationship with the Lord. The leader informed them that Jesus loves them very much and treated some of his special brides differently than all the others. The conversation continued downward from there. The leader told her we should submit to (god) Jesus, totally, because, after all, Jesus is your husband! He wants to reveal and show how much he loves you! Intimately. He wants us to keep it a secret between you and him. Their conversation went a lot further than that including sexual details. I remember in the nineties many older single women who would say, "Jesus is my husband. I don't need anyone else!" One of the women that spoke to me said that she spoke to a pastor's wife about it. She told me that the pastor's wife appeared stunned concerning her complete story and appeared to have no wisdom on the topic. At the time the woman who spoke to me was a professional career person and she was surprised to learn about the lack of awareness in church leadership concerning the issues. She said that she was going to write a short book about it, because women needed to know the truth about this secretly kept demonic deception that women were naively participating in. I became aware that she researched the issue and knew more about the deception then I realized.

The Lord gave me so many divine appointments and He revealed that this issue was also experienced in multiple personalities. That blew my mind in the beginning as He ministered to them setting them free from those sexual intrusion issues. I told the two women that the prayer group participants were deceived, gullible, and possibly desperate to believe such a lie of the enemy. It was also sinful and detestable to the Lord. I encouraged them to inform their pastors. First of all, we are not yet the brides of Jesus yet. We are betrothed to Him at this time or engaged to be His bride. He is coming back for a bride without spot or wrinkle. The marriage did not happen yet. Besides there is no gender in heaven, so there is no sex as on earth. It is written that His love is sufficient and will consume us. There is a false jesus in the spirit. It's a demonic smooth-talking deceiver speaking through your thoughts, especially if you desire and invite It in. This demonic spirit or other seductive spirits will manifest on you, if its continually invited. Its appearance is described in the same way no matter where people come from who have met "it" in the spirit. It has a short red beard, red hair, and cold hands. Since this is the first book that I am writing, I thought I would expose this deceptive secret practice so that others would not be deceived into allowing this to happen to them or anyone else. To those who have been deceived by this sexual (husband) demonic spirit's lies who still have "ears to hear," repent and renounce the false demonic jesus and its work that may be attached to your life. Break the power and renounce all soul-ties and any seeds that was deposited in you from Its intrusion. The seeds may cause a high seductive feeling. Change your ways in this matter. Seek wise council if needed and move on.

After writing about my ministry experience above, I recently found a printed short article titled "What is the bridal paradigm, and is it biblical?" The answer and explanation to this question is found online under; 'Got Questions' "Your Questions, Biblical Answers". In the written article it states "In the paradigm, people are taught to see themselves as "married" to Christ. In some meetings "wedding ceremonies" are held in which individuals speak marriage vows to Jesus and walk under a Chuppah, a Jewish marriage canopy. They are encouraged to participate in a "bridal fast" and are often told to allow themselves to be "ravished" by Jesus. Words such as intimacy, passion, and lovesick are part of the standard vocabulary.

Teachers place a heavy emphasis on highly allegorical interpretation of the Song of Solomon. In their view, the book is more then a depiction of sensual love between a husband and a wife; it's a metaphor of Jesus and the individual believer".

The spiritual world is very real. Unfortunately the enemy (darkness) will deceitfully counterfeit and demoniacally may take advantage of any spiritual door a person unknowingly opens to Its advantage. Then Its deception manifestations continues from there.

Unfortunately, the Church at large is silent or unaware that these are real issues. Leaders of women's prayer groups should expose this spiritual deception. It is written, "My people perish, because of lack of knowledge" (Hosea 4:6). The Church has a responsibility to spiritually protect its members and the children of God at large. Jesus would run after just one lost deceived sheep bringing them back, keeping them safe from the mouths of the dark wolfs.

CHAPTER 35

MULTIPLE PERSONALITIES AND SEDUCTIVE SEXUAL SPIRITS

In this chapter:
- A Brief Understanding of Multiple Personalities and Why or How They Develop

A person who exhibits multiple personalities disorders, knowingly or unknowingly may encounter demonic spiritual sexual abuse assaults against one or more of their personalities (parts) in their sleep. Their natural bodies may experience the aftermath or the sexual abuse encounter confusing the person of its unknown origin. Many times a person can have uncontrollable sexual recurring nightmares. They don't realize a seductive spirit found a spiritual open door in them or through the alter personality (part). A person may not believe this is possible, until the demonic seductive spirit is confronted. Then the person's beliefs are completely changed.

A Brief Understanding of Multiple Personalities and Why or How They Develop

Multiple personalities in brief, are originally created by a horrific trauma or an extreme emotional experience that happened to a person. It may be hard to accept or mentally process to cope with its reality. The highly intense stressful thoughts of the person may switch the mind to protection mode by blocking, hiding, or burying the negative emotional trauma deep in the mind as if the incident never happened. The person will not remember experiencing the emotional or physical trauma. It is an unconscious form of denial that the mind initiates. This disorder is more common than people may believe. Simple denial seems to be commonplace and recognized to an extent during personal ministry. But I'm speaking about the upper scale of traumatic experiential denial and its common hidden coping design that may expose itself during personal ministry. Each person who lives with this disorder is usually misdiagnosed. The usual symptoms are, moodiness, (many different moods that change regularly for no apparent reason), confusion (forgetting or acting confused concerning current or past conversations or actions), and whispering or mumbling (unknowingly speaking out verbally, or quietly to themselves, speaking a few words or a full sentence, but they don't remember or deny that they spoke anything when you ask them what they said). If they feel very happy or afraid, they may briefly speak like a child and at times exhibit low brief sounds of crying. A more severe condition is when the person starts to lose time. An example of this is when they tell a family member that they are taking a quick trip to the store and will be right back. Then they are gone four or five hours before they return. When they are questioned where they were for four hours they will argue that they were only gone for twenty minutes. When they realized they were actually gone four hours, they get nervous and panicky not understanding what's happening to them. They can't account for or remember what else they did during that time. This happens because a different personality (mood) came up and took over for the other three hours doing other things unknown to the person and everybody else.

The question I frequently get asked is, how do these personalities develop? They can begin with an experienced trauma, an intense emotional experience, personal or sexual abuse, abandonment, or rejection with malice. These experienced highly emotional issues that the mind hides or blocks from a person's conscience mind in order to cope in reality, I call "individual emotional hidden Hurts". These "Hurts" are each arranged in the mind systematically and are categorized separately from one another in the mind. The "Hurts" individually becomes or are called "Parts". Each "Part" is connected with only one "Hurt'. The "Hurt" and the "Part" become ONE, resulting in the development of a "personality, sometimes described as dis-association." A "Hurt", "Part," and "Personality" are synonymous with each other when you are ministering to a person with multiple personalities. The intensity and the extent of the trauma experienced and the measure of their inability to cope will determine how many personalities may develop in the mind. Again, each personality is considered to be one "Part" which carries or hides one emotional/ psychological "Hurt" that expresses itself differently in each "Personality." One personality only carries experiences of one hurt, keeping that experience hidden from the acknowledgment of the person who experienced the trauma. This may sound confusing, but it is very simple to understand as you work with people that developed this issue. Each talking personality has a name, an age and a particular purpose that becomes exposed and realized during ministry. Each time the person has an additional trauma, it becomes easier to subconsciously deny the experience which may cause another personality to develop as a coping device. Usually, medication has no healing affect other than partial sedation to lessen the effects of active moods that the personalities may exhibit. Medication does not integrate the personalities. Healing is needed for each personality individually. It's important to realize that each personality has their own beliefs, thoughts, value system, and problems that may be totally inconsistent with the person that suffered the trauma. The personalities are separated in the mind and unable to see or meet one another. They are only able to distinguish one another by the sound of their voices. Sometimes their outwardly spoken voice can be slightly to extremely different from one another. The personalities are NOT demons, although some angry personalities for many reasons may be demonically influenced.

Now let's go a little deeper to understand the environment of the personalities. True healing becomes a 90% spiritual issue which is why medication is unsuccessful. In brief, the personalities, although hidden in the mind, are exposed and live in the spirit world to an extent which creates another issue. Demonic entities, including people who astral project with evil intentions, may badger, torment, or sexually abuse a personality(part) in the spirit. The person may experience the aftermath feeling in the natural. They may also experience any side effects and feelings of the abuse when that abused personality pops up and becomes active in the person's life even if it's for a few hours a day. This causes a lot of confusion and concern, because they don't know what caused the feelings or the aftermath. When that personality goes down and a different one pops up usually the switch is not noticed. This other personality carries a different hurt or mood, and it may not remember anything from the former conversation. Possibly because they didn't hear it, even if it was only a few minutes earlier. To achieve healing the person ministering has to first develop a trusting relationship with the person and then with the parts/personalities so that they would feel comfortable communicating with you. It's also important to learn to recognize the sign or gesture that the person uses just before the personality changes/switches. An example of this subtle sign may be scratching their arm, head or chin or a yawn, cough, blink of their eyes, or headache, a five- seconds or more nap, or a short pain somewhere.

Usually the sign/gesture between all the personality changes (or switches) in that particular person is the same. You have to observe the person and watch to identify it. Typically, the person is unaware of the sign they portray and I wouldn't inform them about it. This way you will know that a different personality may have come up. Sometimes a demonic entity may pop up (showing no sign of the change) disguising itself as a personality. It even tries to talk with the same voice of the personality to deceive you. They usually speak very little as they observe their surroundings and tries to avoid eye contact. They usually only stay up for a few minutes. If they feel pressured to answer your questions, they will abruptly and angrily speak with their own creepy voice vulgar nasty things. Usually after they expose themselves, they go back down into hiding. The person will usually be totally unaware of the demonic entity's short visit.

Living in denial of life's negative traumatic circumstances that a person may unfortunately experience enables the person to live blissfully unaware of the fact that they carry an extensive amount of unsettled (unresolved) emotional hidden trauma. Of course, this is not a healthy way to live. Multiple personalities orchestrated by our minds in part is an effective denial blocker. But obviously it has many side effects especially when the hidden negative experiences start to leak out to the person's conscious mind. The real trouble starts when the tragic memories start to slip into their nightly dreams and unwanted confusing daily flashbacks start to occur. Suddenly one or more personalities start to come apart and become disruptive. The person may start to hear the real uncontrollable voices of the parts/personalities speaking/crying/screaming in their head concerning their emotional hurts/ and pain which is actually the person themselves. The voice or voices that they hear actually speaking/ or crying in their heads is not demonic although at times it could be demonically influenced, but not likely at this stage. It is one of the personalities emotional pain that is being leaked out or exposed to the person's (now) conscious mind. It's the stored hidden trauma memory that feels emotionally fresh even though the actual trauma incident could have occurred five, ten, twenty or more years ago. There's an easy process of awareness and healing as the personalities are brought out into the light. It's important to work with one part at a time. I work with the (one) personality (hurt) that is now being exposed by revealing the cause of the emotional pain that the "part" was carrying and protecting from the person's memory. Together we resolve the personality's troubled issues through forgiveness, as Jesus leads, completing the healing necessary to restore wholeness to the person. As that process comes to an end that personality disappears and integrates as one in the person. Peace is achieved concerning that one personality through Christ Jesus, the True Great Physician.

To minister to a person with multiple personalities it's not necessary to wait for a major disruption to happen. Once recognized the person can receive ministry by allowing the Lord to bring up the "Parts" (personalities) individually, bringing them into His light of truth. Then we go from there and follow the Lord's established plan. It's common that the Lord integrates the personality as healing and oneness occurs without the person knowing about it. The Lord leads the complete release as I participate and observe.

The worst thing the person can do is go to a hospital and say that they hear screaming voices in their heads. They will be diagnosed with a terrible label and prescribed heavy meds. Unfortunately, most of the church is clueless on how to minister effectively in this arena, even though it's a major spiritual issue.

This information is simplified. It is just revealing the surface. I will explain in precise detail in the book that I'm writing concerning releasing people with multiple personality disorders. It will bring you into the mind of the person with the multiple personality and how they become healed and free, reaping wholeness. This is regardless if the person has 2 personalities or 60 talking personalities. There are many parts that have no voice to communicate, but that's another story that will be explained in the book. There is a process to meet and work with each personality individually, as they each come forward in their mental coping captivity into the light and truth. In a short time, becoming completely free and whole again, as a one mind person. Psychology does not have a clue on how to achieve this healing outcome. This is a drug-free, quick process verses prolonged psychological care. For people who have scary reoccurring nightmares the healing process is similar.

Everything that I have learned and written about releasing multiple personalities into wholeness, I give the Lord Jesus Christ all the credit. He is the One who does the complete ministry, using and teaching me as His facilitator. Twenty-five years ago, is when He gave me a divine appointment in this area of ministry. It took four months then to achieve the same results in less than two hours today. Eventually complete healing (in and through Him) will manifest itself with a spoken WORD (His word). I believe I will experience that very soon.

NOTES

CHAPTER 36

A REVELATION CONCERNING FORGIVENESS THAT WILL CHANGE YOUR LIFE

In this chapter:
- Overcoming Repetitive Forgiveness Prayers and Replacing It With Peace
- A Spiritual Prayer Spoken With Authority Reaps Continuous Victory in Areas of Forgiveness
- Another Forgiveness Victory to Catch in Your Heart

This is another personal Holy Spirit experience, a true story, giving you great spiritual insight on how to achieve victory when confronted with the issue of needing to forgive someone over and over again for the same original offense.

Overcoming Repetitive Forgiveness Prayers and Replacing It With Peace

I gave a message in a church consisting of about 300 people concerning the issue of repetitive forgiveness prayer. I asked the congregation not to reveal their answers openly, but to only think of their response at the time.

The questions were: 1. How many people have forgiven someone who physically, mentally or sexually abused you? Some of you may have been abandoned, rejected, cheated, or the victim of adultery. 2. How many times upon hearing the name of your abuser(s) or smelling their cologne/perfume, or thinking you saw them or someone who looks like them, does the same sick feeling return? Does a familiar troubling emotional memory pop up again even if the offenses were 5,10 or 20 years ago? This past negative experience gradually consumes your thoughts and heart so much that you feel you need to forgive them all over again. You try to rid the emotional hurt, anger, disappointment or a sin committed against you. Again, the same scenario leads you to releasing the person through a prayer of forgiveness in the Lord. Sometimes people battle with these negative emotional feelings that are triggered for years, maybe a lifetime. Some people take medication because they don't want to experience or feel the painful memory anymore. 3. How many of you are in this predicament? Feeling the need to forgive the same person many times over for the same offence as reminders come up. Sometimes it may be receiving and accepting forgiveness for oneself!

I asked them to raise their hands if this is their experience. To my surprise, more than half the people raised their hands. There were probably many others that felt embarrassed or self-conscience and didn't raise their hand.

Before I was saved, I lived with my girlfriend for about two years. Although we were busy, we rarely argued and had common goals. One day I came home and most of her stuff was gone. There was a note on the table saying, "I will call you later tonight." She didn't call me for two days. My heart ached as I waited for her call wondering where she was and why she left. At the time I owned and ran a seasonal tree business. Like most workaholic's I worked long hours and took advantage of the good weather before winter season arrived.

She stopped by my house three days later unexpectedly and took the rest of her stuff. She told me she needed a break and rented a room from a family close by. It was amazing and sad what I learned about the situation a few days later. She moved in with an older guy whom she had been secretly seeing for four months. The late nights she was supposedly at work were really spent with him. There were two separate times she traveled out-of-state to supposedly see her family and she was with this guy. I trusted her and never thought she would do something like this. I was totally shocked and devastated as I thought about her smooth deceptions during the prior four months.

The Lord used this incident to draw me to Himself (James 4:8). After a month of working through my new reality, I had to forgive her to stop the negative repetitive tape playing in my head. It took three months for the Lord to replace the tape with Himself. He began to reveal Himself in a tangible way as I kept my eyes and heart focused on Him.

Every two to three months, as I explained earlier, if I smelled her perfume, thought I saw her, or heard the familiar sound of her voice, or heard someone say her name, thoughts would suddenly pop-up: I can't believe she did that to me; she was seeing him for four months; she lied about her work and long weekends; I can't believe she had secret plans. Eventually I felt the anger rising. I didn't like that feeling, so I forgave her again speaking out loudly before the Lord. I went through the same thing about every three months. I would totally surrender and forgive her again as I experienced little reminders of her. At the end of the second year after she left, I was driving on the interstate and a car that looked like hers was passing on my right. I looked over to see if it was her. It wasn't. This triggered the same flood of thoughts and questions over again. I heard my thoughts say, remember what she did to you. I responded to my own thoughts saying, "I can't believe she did that and lied to me." Then I heard that she even moved in with him. I responded to my thoughts again saying, "I can't believe she moved in with that guy." Then my thought said, "She took secret romantic trips with him." I responded to my thoughts again saying, "I can't believe she took short trips with him using her work as a lying excuse." I was experiencing all these mixed hurtful negative emotions. Then suddenly the anger feeling started to pop up that I didn't like, so I turned to the Lord to forgive her again. As I was driving, I started to forgive her out loud, again! Then in an instant, I realized this was stupid and told the Lord that obviously I can't forgive her. I don't know how to. Even though I believed I did forgive her, something would always remind me of her and what she did. All of the negative experiences, emotions and thoughts would flood my mind again.

A Spiritual Prayer Spoken with Authority Reaps Continuous Victory in Areas of Forgiveness

Then the Lord gave me a revealing download. He clearly showed me an animated quick vision of what was happening in the spirit and how to deal with it. I thought "Very Cool". The results changed my life and taught me a secret concerning forgiveness as I continued driving. In the vision I clearly saw this large brown colored snake wrapped around me. Its head was about a foot wide and was arched back and was speaking in my right ear. I realized I was responding to the snake's voice as if they were my own thoughts. What a revelation!

It was actually the enemy speaking in my ear causing me to think they were my thoughts. As my emotions were stirred up, the snake would bite me on my shoulder which was the real cause of the poisonous anger popping up. The Lord showed me this clearly. The best part is what the Lord told me to say to the evil snake and its hidden cohort friends. The experience and the results I now understand and own in my spiritual prayer life and ministry. I have revealed this secret spiritual tormentor to many others that have been emotionally trapped by this hidden deception, setting them totally free to move forward in their life.

I confronted the snake in the authority of Jesus and His righteous anger. The Lord totally Hates darkness because It draws people's hearts away from Him and His truth. I asked the Lord's voice to speak through me in the spirit world confronting the darkness. I said, "In the name of Jesus Christ of Nazareth, I command all of the darkness and Its cohorts that come to speak or torment me concerning this issue with Mary to hear what I speak right now, and I rebuke any disobedience in Jesus' name. I forgive Mary for everything, I release her and set her free THROUGH the blood of Jesus Christ of Nazareth. If you have anything else to speak to me concerning this issue, I command you to go directly to Jesus Christ first. I have given everything concerning Mary to Him. I know that you can NOT speak to me THROUGH the blood of Jesus and you can NOT come to me THROUGH the blood of Jesus concerning this issue anymore!

Wow! Instantly it became so quiet. I thought my car radio shut off. I reached over to turn the radio volume, but then I realized the radio wasn't on. At that moment I realized that all the noise and busyness was in my head and now it was totally silent. It was an unbelievable experience!

I couldn't stop thinking about what just happened. After five minutes of continued silence, I told the Lord that I know I shouldn't test Him, but I had to test myself to see what was going to happen because of what I just experienced. I purposely tried to hate her. I tried to bring up every negative thought and emotion concerning her and heard and felt nothing. I tried intensely again but still couldn't conjure up any negative thoughts or emotional feelings concerning her. It felt like I was trying to hate a blank piece of paper laying on the ground. Nothing, absolutely nothing came up. In fact, I started to feel annoyed at myself trying to conjure up negative feelings or emotions when there was nothing there, even though there was a flood of them present fifteen minutes earlier. Totally Amazing!!!

I told the Lord that I'm trying to hate her, but I can't, and I don't have any interest in even thinking about her. Over my thoughts I could hear the Lord say, "If you truly forgive someone, you can't hate them." This true forgiveness revelation command prayer understanding totally changed my life and filled me with His peace. It continually enables me to walk in true forgiveness practicing my authority in Christ Jesus by shutting down accusing dark voices from speaking to my thoughts, now that I'm fully aware of Its secret tactics.

I am thankful and astonished because this prayer is always effective. It works with big and small issues that forgiveness is needed for. Don't let the enemy deceive and convince you that it won't work for you. Remember to always ask the Holy Spirit to teach you how to pray effectively and follow His heartfelt instructions.

IMPORTANT - The Lord forgives you for everything that you ask Him to forgive. The enemy is the accuser of the brethren and will torment you concerning issues you are already forgiven for and have forgiven others for. It knows you're forgiven, but It uses its secret spiritual back door "voice" to accuse and torment you through your thoughts in the spirit. Its where your battles are fought and won, through the Victorious Warrior Jesus Christ who hopefully resides in you. If you're not totally sure, then speak out and believe the salvation prayer #1+ #2 found in the Appendix.

Another Forgiveness Victory to Catch in Your Heart

Years ago, I had many employees including family members. Some of them were rough characters. Looking back, I realize that the Lord used these guys to help train me in the things of the spirit. A couple of them had short fuses and when they disagreed or became angry, they at times would curse and yell at me. On occasion it would get so bad that I wouldn't want to talk or be around them for a couple days. One day the Holy Spirit reminded me of the strategy from the previous story.

Now, if I have a disagreement or argument with someone where an offense develops, even if the person is right, but responds in an offensive tone or action, my response is to do the following:

When the verbal confrontation is over, I walk away. I whisper out, "In the name of Jesus Christ of Nazareth, I break the power of all the negative words that the person just spoke to me. I don't receive them and I proclaim the blood of Jesus over all of them from attaching to my heart. I command them all to fall to the ground powerless and not to resurrect in Jesus' name." I say this while swiping my hand from my heart in a downward motion removing any negative words received to the ground. Then I speak out or whisper, "I command any spirits of darkness that want to pick up this offense to torment me, I command you to hear what I speak, right now! I rebuke any disobedience in Jesus name". "I forgive, release and set them free THROUGH the blood of Jesus, in Jesus' name. If you have anything else to speak to me concerning this issue, I command you to go directly to Jesus Christ first, because I have given it all to Him. I know you cannot speak to me THROUGH the blood of Jesus and you cannot come THROUGH His blood to me."

After I say that command prayer, I can see the person who offended me two hours later and talk to them without feeling any negative emotions, even if I try and think about the conflict. Otherwise, the spoken offence may take a much longer time to forgive and release them, possibly giving the enemy an open door to torment me.

JESUS GIVES THE GREAT COMMISSION

Matthew 28:18-20

[18] Then Jesus came to them and said, "All authority in heaven and on earth has been given to me. [19] Therefore go and make disciples of all nations, baptizing them in the name of the Father and of the Son and of the Holy Spirit, [20] and teaching them to obey everything I have commanded you. And surely I am with you always, to the very end of the age."

THREE OTHER COMMISSIONS

Mark 16:15-18

[15] He said to them, "Go into all the world and preach the gospel to all creation. [16] Whoever believes and is baptized will be saved, but whoever does not believe will be condemned. [17] And these signs will accompany those who believe: In my name they will drive out demons; they will speak in new tongues; [18] they will pick up snakes with their hands; and when they drink deadly poison, it will not hurt them at all; they will place their hands on sick people, and they will get well."

Luke 24:45-49

[45] Then he opened their minds so they could understand the Scriptures. [46] He told them, "This is what is written: The Messiah will suffer and rise from the dead on the third day, [47] and repentance for the forgiveness of sins will (should) be preached in his name to all nations, beginning at Jerusalem. [48] You are witnesses of these things. [49] I am going to send you what my Father has promised; but stay in the city until you have been clothed with power from on high."

John 20:21-22

[21] Again Jesus said, "Peace be with you! As the Father has sent me, I am sending you." [22] And with that he breathed on them and said, "Receive the Holy Spirit. [23] If you forgive anyone's sins, their sins are forgiven; if you do not forgive them, they are not forgiven."

APPENDIX

Salvation Prayer

Part 1: Lord Jesus, come into my heart. Be my Lord and Savior. Forgive me for all of my sins, even the hidden sins in my heart that I'm not aware of and fill me with your Holy Spirit, right now, in Jesus' name.

Part 2: And I command any and all spirits of darkness who come to torment me in any way to hear what I speak right now in the name of Jesus Christ of Nazareth and I rebuke any disobedience. I rebuke and renounce all spirits of darkness and their cohorts that I have invited upon myself knowingly and unknowingly. I don't want you anymore. I don't need you anymore, I renounce you and command you to leave all parts of my life and go directly to Jesus Christ of Nazareth for Him to deal with you. I command you never to return to my life in Jesus' name. Jesus Christ of Nazareth is my new Lord and Master. And I give you, Lord, permission to remove anything that is not of you.

Forgiveness Prayer
(To be whispered or spoken out loud)

Father, in the name of Jesus Christ of Nazareth, I forgive <<insert person's name>> for << take time to speak out everything the person did or said against you>>. I forgive them. I release them and I set them free **through** the blood of Jesus Christ of Nazareth. Speak the following out loud with authority and heart-felt righteous anger. And I command all the darkness and its cohorts that come to torment and speak to me concerning this issue to hear what I speak right now in the name of Jesus Christ of Nazareth, and I rebuke any disobedience. I have forgiven and released <<insert name>> and I have set them free **through** the blood of Jesus Christ of Nazareth!

I have given everything to Jesus concerning them and this issue. If you have anything else to speak to me concerning this issue, I command you to go speak directly to Jesus Christ of Nazareth first, because I know you can NOT speak to me through His blood and you can NOT come to me **through** the blood of Jesus Christ concerning this issue anymore. Amen!

www.ingramcontent.com/pod-product-compliance
Lightning Source LLC
Chambersburg PA
CBHW080840120626
46553CB00009B/2508